Chocolate Cookies

Also by Lorraine Bodger

Great American Cookies
Great American Cakes
The Christmas Kitchen
Chicken Dinners
The Complete Vegetable Cookbook
Savory Tarts
Chutneys and Relishes
Sweet and Savory Sauces

Chocolate Cookies

53 chewy, crunchy, rich,
dunkable chocolate cookies
every chocoholic will love

Lorraine Bodger
Illustrations by Lorraine Bodger

ST. MARTIN'S GRIFFIN
NEW YORK

Design by Maureen Troy

Library of Congress Cataloging-in-Publication Data

Bodger, Lorraine.
    Chocolate cookies : 53 chewy, crunchy, rich, dunkable
chocolate cookies every chocoholic will love / Lorraine Bodger.—
1st ed.
        p.   cm.
    ISBN 0-312-18707-6
    1. Cookies.   2. Cookery (Chocolate)   I. Title
TX772.B62   1998   98-11978
641.8'654—dc21   CIP

First Edition: June 1998
10 9 8 7 6 5 4 3 2 1

Contents

Chocolate Cookies

Making Chocolate Cookies

$\sim \circlearrowright \circlearrowright \sim$

The following tips and guidelines will help you to bake the best possible chocolate cookies. If you're an experienced cookie baker, you're probably already familiar with many of these suggestions. If you're new to cookie baking, all the essential information you need is right here.

- Read the entire recipe before you start baking.
- Use high-quality ingredients, including the best chocolate you can afford (see page 5 for advice on chocolate).
- Unless otherwise specified, use unsalted (sweet) butter, all-purpose flour, white granulated sugar, large eggs, and ground spices. Nuts must be absolutely fresh or your cookies will be ruined; the taste of stale or moldy nuts can't be concealed. Raisins and other dried fruit should be soft. Vanilla extract must be the real thing—no imitations. The same goes for chocolate—no chocolate-flavored products; be sure to read the section on chocolate on page 5.
- In these recipes, there's no need to sift flour before measuring it.
- Measure ingredients carefully. For liquids, use clear glass or plastic measuring cups; for dry ingredients, use metal cups or measuring spoons that can be leveled off with a knife or spatula.
- To measure dry ingredients (flour, granulated sugar, confectioners'

sugar, cocoa), spoon into a metal measuring cup and level off with a knife or spatula. To measure light or dark brown sugar, pack it so firmly into a metal measuring cup that it holds its shape when turned out.

- Use shiny—not dark—baking sheets (also called cookie sheets) that fit on the oven rack with at least two inches between each edge of the baking sheet and the adjacent wall of the oven, so the heat can circulate freely. Have two baking sheets—one to go in the oven while you prepare the second. If you need extras, use jelly roll pans or inverted baking pans.

- Cookies should be baked in the center of the oven, so shift one oven rack to the center slot.

- Preheat the oven for 10 to 15 minutes. Be sure your oven temperature is correct; if it isn't, the baking time given in the recipes won't be reliable.

- For best results, check the oven temperature often by putting a mercury-type oven thermometer in the middle of a rack placed in the center slot of the oven; preheat the oven for 15 minutes and check the thermometer. If the temperature setting disagrees with the reading on the thermometer, adjust it up or down accordingly.

- To grease and flour a baking sheet, first use a pastry brush to apply a thin coat of soft butter or margarine to the baking sheet. Then sprinkle all over with flour and (working over the sink) tap the sheet briskly while you tilt it back and forth. Tip the excess flour into the sink.

- Use an electric mixer for creaming butter and sugar; beat until the sugar is barely grainy. This can take a few minutes, so be patient.

- Set your kitchen timer when you put a sheet of cookies into the oven. The baking times given in the recipes have been carefully tested, so if one baking time is given, set your timer for that number. If a choice of times is given in the recipe (for example, 8 to 10 minutes), set the timer for the lower number and check the cookies when the timer goes off.

• When making batches of cookies, it's not necessary to wash each baking sheet every time you reuse it. Just scrape off crumbs and wipe with a paper towel. Be sure the baking sheet is cool before you grease it or put more cookie dough on it.

• When cookies are done, let them cool as instructed in the recipe. Loosen them all at the same time with a metal spatula and transfer to wire racks, making a single layer of cookies. Don't pile up or store the cookies until they are completely cool. (You'll find cookie storage information on page 87.)

• If your baked cookies cool too long on the baking sheet and become stuck, return the sheet to the oven for a minute or so; they should loosen up. Remove and cool them as usual.

Handy Measurements

Pinch = a little less than ⅛ teaspoon

⅛ teaspoon = 2 pinches

1 tablespoon = 3 teaspoons

¼ cup = 4 tablespoons

⅓ cup = 5⅓ tablespoons

¼ cup = 4 tablespoons

⅓ cup = 5⅓ tablespoons

¼ cup = 4 tablespoons

1 cup = 16 tablespoons

¼ cup butter = ½ stick = 4 tablespoons

½ cup butter = ¼ pound = 1 stick = 8 tablespoons

1 cup butter = ½ pound = 2 sticks = 16 tablespoons

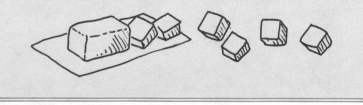

All About Chocolate

*A*s with all ingredients, it makes sense to use the best you can afford, and using high-quality chocolate will make an enormous difference in the taste of your cookies. Premium brands of chocolate (such as Callebaut, Lindt, Tobler, Valrhona, and Ghirardelli) can be found in gourmet shops and other fine food stores. Baker's, Dove, Hershey's, and Nestlé are widely available in supermarkets and groceries.

The following information and techniques are all you need to know about chocolate when you're making chocolate cookies.

• The recipes in this book were tested with Callebaut chocolate when melted chocolate was required, and with Nestlé's regular and miniature semisweet chocolate chips when chips were required.

• Whichever brand of chocolate you opt for, be sure it's the real thing; never use chocolate-flavored products.

• The chocolates most often called for in these recipes are *semisweet* and *unsweetened.* When you see them in the ingredients list, use blocks, bars, or squares of either premium or regular chocolate. Store chocolate in a cool, dry place (not the refrigerator).

• Use packaged semisweet chocolate chips only when chips are required in a recipe; do not substitute them for fine chocolate when *semisweet chocolate, melted* is listed as an ingredient.

• There are several ways to melt chocolate—in the oven, in the microwave, in the top of a double boiler, in a metal bowl set over a saucepan containing an inch or two of boiling water, or in a heavy saucepan over very low heat.

All of these methods are excellent, but for cookie baking I like to keep things simple by using the heavy saucepan method. First, coarsely chop the chocolate. Put the pieces into the heavy saucepan and set it on the stove over very low heat. Stir the chocolate constantly until it is about half-melted, then remove the saucepan from the heat and continue stirring until the chocolate is completely melted and smooth. (This guarantees that the chocolate won't burn.) Set aside until cool.

• Chocolate has one peculiar quality: It can be melted *with* liquid, but even a drop of liquid added to already-melted chocolate may cause it to "seize," which means to clump and harden. If this happens, throw out the seized chocolate and begin again; the recommended remedies rarely correct the problem.

• When cocoa powder is listed in the ingredients, use pure, unsweetened cocoa powder; do not use cocoa mix. Alkalized (Dutch-process) and nonalkalized cocoa powder work equally well in cookie baking.

Equipment Checklist

- ❑ Graduated measuring cups for dry ingredients
- ❑ Glass measuring cup for liquid ingredients
- ❑ Measuring spoons
- ❑ Small and large mixing bowls
- ❑ Heavy saucepan for melting chocolate
- ❑ Wooden spoons for mixing by hand
- ❑ Wire whisk
- ❑ Electric mixer with variable speeds (hand-held is fine)
- ❑ Rubber spatulas for scraping down the sides of the bowls
- ❑ Oven thermometer (mercury type) for checking and adjusting oven temperature
- ❑ Timer
- ❑ Baking sheets (shiny, not dark)
- ❑ Jelly roll pan for bar cookies and to use as an extra baking sheet
- ❑ Baking pans in standard sizes for bar cookies
- ❑ Metal spatula or pancake turner for removing cookies
- ❑ Wire racks, raised on wire feet, for cooling the cookies
- ❑ Rolling pin
- ❑ Cookie cutters
- ❑ Cookie press with an assortment of disks
- ❑ Pastry bag with a few large and small tips
- ❑ Food processor (optional)

Drop Cookies

Drop cookies are the quickest and easiest cookies to make. Simply scoop up the dough with a teaspoon or tablespoon (as called for in the recipe), push it off the spoon onto a baking sheet (using your finger or another teaspoon), and pop the baking sheet into a preheated oven.

Tip: Keep the size of the drops uniform so that all the cookies bake evenly and in the same amount of time.

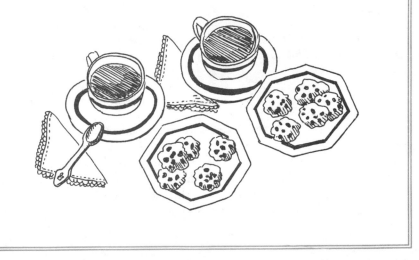

Mountaintops

Here's a batch of crunchy cookies with a variety of chopped nuts mixed into the dough. The tops are garnished with Vanilla Glaze and sweet coconut, so they look a bit like snow-capped mountains.

1 cup flour
½ teaspoon baking powder
½ teaspoon salt
½ cup (1 stick) unsalted butter,
    at room temperature
1 cup sugar
2 eggs
2 teaspoons vanilla extract
3 ounces unsweetened chocolate,
    melted and cooled

2 cups chopped nuts (walnuts, pecans,
    almonds, unsalted peanuts, or
    any combination of these)
Vanilla Glaze (recipe
    on page 120)

Note: Place a piece of plastic wrap
directly on the glaze to prevent
the formation of a crust.

1 to 1½ cups (about 4 ounces)
    shredded sweetened coconut

1. Preheat the oven to 350°F; grease 1 or 2 baking sheets. In a small bowl, stir or whisk together the flour, baking powder, and salt.

2. In a large bowl, cream the butter and sugar. Add the eggs, vanilla, and melted chocolate and beat until well blended. Gradually add the flour mixture, blending well after each addition. Stir in the chopped nuts.

3. Drop the dough by rounded teaspoons, 1 inch apart, onto the prepared baking sheet.

4. Bake for 12 minutes. Leave the cookies on the baking sheet. While the cookies are still hot, top each one with a generous half teaspoon of Vanilla Glaze; it will melt and spread. While the glaze is still warm and tacky, press a big pinch of shredded coconut on it. Transfer the cookies to wire racks to finish cooling. Store only when the glaze is firm.

• *Makes about 4½ dozen cookies*

How to Toast Nuts

Spread whole or chopped nuts—almonds, hazelnuts, walnuts, or pecans—on a jelly roll pan or other pan with sides (nuts will slide off a baking sheet) and place in a preheated 350°F oven for 5 to 10 minutes. When the nuts smell toasty and a *cooled* nut is crisp and crunchy, the nuts are ready. Be sure to watch carefully to avoid burning. (Keep in mind that chopped nuts toast more quickly than whole nuts.) Let the nuts cool in the pan on a wire rack.

To remove the papery skins of toasted hazelnuts (as much as will come off), rub a few hazelnuts at a time between your palms or in a rough dish towel.

Tip: If almonds must be blanched (skinned) before toasting, put them in a pot of boiling water for a minute or so, then drain and rinse in cold water; pinch off the brown skins.

Easy Chocolate-Fruit Cookies

This combination will surprise and delight you—a light chocolate cookie with a hint of cinnamon, lots of plump currants, and chopped apricots. A bit of sugar topping adds a pretty look.

1½ cups flour	1 cup packed light brown sugar
½ teaspoon baking powder	2 eggs
½ teaspoon baking soda	2 ounces semisweet chocolate,
¼ teaspoon salt	melted and cooled
½ teaspoon cinnamon	½ cup currants
½ cup (1 stick) unsalted butter,	½ cup chopped dried apricots
at room temperature	Sugar for topping

1. Preheat the oven to 350°F; grease 1 or 2 baking sheets. In a small bowl, stir or whisk together the flour, baking powder, baking soda, salt, and cinnamon.

2. In a large bowl, cream the butter and brown sugar. Add the eggs and melted chocolate and beat until well blended. Gradually add the flour mixture, blending well after each addition. Stir in the currants and apricots.

3. Drop the dough by rounded teaspoons, 2 inches apart, onto the prepared baking sheet. Flatten each drop slightly, using a finger dipped in granulated sugar.

Bake for 12 to 13 minutes. Let the cookies cool on the baking sheet for 1 minute, then transfer to wire racks to finish cooling. When they cool, the cookies will be thin and crisp, about 2½ inches in diameter.

• *Makes about 4½ dozen cookies*

Chocolate-Cashew Drop Cookies

Brown sugar and chopped cashews give these small cookies a toasty flavor. Note that the recipe makes lots of cookies for munching.

1½ cups flour
½ teaspoon baking soda
¼ teaspoon salt
½ cup (1 stick) unsalted butter,
  at room temperature
1 cup packed light brown sugar

2 eggs
1 teaspoon vanilla extract
3 ounces unsweetened chocolate,
  melted and cooled
½ cup chopped unsalted roasted cashews
72 (or more) toasted cashew halves

Note: A 7-ounce jar of cashews contains more than enough for both the chopped cashews and the cashew halves.

1. Preheat the oven to 350°F; grease 1 or 2 baking sheets. In a small bowl, stir or whisk together the flour, baking soda, and salt.

2. In a large bowl, cream the butter and brown sugar. Add the eggs, vanilla, and melted chocolate and beat until well blended. Gradually add the flour mixture, blending well after each addition. Stir in the chopped cashews.

3. Drop the dough by rounded teaspoons, 1 inch apart, onto the prepared baking sheet. Firmly press a cashew half (flat side up) onto the top of each cookie.

4. Bake for 11 minutes. Let the cookies cool on the baking sheet for 1 or 2 minutes, then transfer to wire racks to finish cooling.

- *Makes about 6 dozen small cookies*

Chocolate–Chocolate Chip Cookies

Can't get enough chocolate? These craggy nuggets should help solve the problem, and the recipe can be doubled if needed. Quick and easy.

¾ cup (1½ sticks) unsalted butter, at room temperature
1½ cups sugar
1 egg
1½ teaspoons vanilla extract

3 ounces unsweetened chocolate, melted and cooled
1¾ cups flour stirred with ¼ teaspoon salt
¾ cup semisweet chocolate chips or chunks
¾ cup chopped pecans or walnuts, toasted

1. Preheat the oven to 350°F; grease 1 or 2 baking sheets.

2. In a large bowl, cream the butter and sugar. Add the egg, vanilla, and melted chocolate and beat until well blended. Gradually add the flour, blending well after each addition. Stir in the chocolate chips and chopped nuts.

3. Drop the cookies by slightly rounded tablespoons, 1 inch apart, onto the prepared baking sheet.

4. Bake for 14 minutes, watching carefully to be sure the bottoms don't burn; the cookies will be slightly soft in the center when removed from the oven. Let the cookies cool on the cookie sheet for 5 minutes, then transfer to wire racks to finish cooling.

• *Makes about 4 dozen cookies*

Chocolate-Oatmeal Crispies

These small crunchy cookies have a light oatmeal flavor. For a tasty variation, add half a cup (or more) of chopped walnuts or pecans to the dough.

1 cup flour
1¼ cups quick (1-minute) oatmeal, uncooked
½ teaspoon baking powder
½ teaspoon salt
½ cup (1 stick) unsalted butter,
 at room temperature

¼ cup sugar
¾ cup packed dark brown sugar
1 egg
1 teaspoon vanilla extract
2 ounces semisweet chocolate,
 melted and cooled

1. Preheat the oven to 350°F; grease 1 or 2 baking sheets. In a small bowl, stir or whisk together the flour, oatmeal, baking powder, and salt.

2. In a large bowl, cream the butter, sugar, and brown sugar. Add the egg, vanilla, and melted chocolate and beat until well blended. Gradually add the flour mixture, blending well after each addition. The dough will be thick.

3. Drop the dough by rounded teaspoons, 1½ inches apart, onto the prepared baking sheet.

4. Bake for 12 to 13 minutes, until the cookies have spread and are dry on top. Immediately transfer the cookies from the baking sheet to wire racks to cool.

- *Makes about 3½ dozen cookies*

Rocky Road Drop Cookies

$\backsim\backsim\backsim$

Heavenly big cookies chock-full of nuts, chocolate chips (white or semi-sweet), and miniature marshmallows. They're total indulgences, crisp on top, gooey and chewy on the inside.

½ cup flour
½ teaspoon baking powder
⅛ teaspoon salt
3 ounces unsweetened chocolate, chopped
6 ounces semisweet chocolate, chopped
6 tablespoons (¾ stick) unsalted butter
3 eggs, at room temperature

1½ cups sugar
1½ teaspoons vanilla extract
1 cup coarsely chopped toasted pecans
1 cup miniature marshmallows
1 cup chopped white chocolate or
   1 cup semisweet chocolate chips

1. Preheat the oven to 350°F; grease and flour 1 or 2 baking sheets. In a small bowl, stir together the flour, baking powder, and salt. In a heavy saucepan over low heat, melt and stir the unsweetened chocolate, semisweet chocolate, and butter until smooth and blended; set aside to cool.

2. In a large bowl, beat together the eggs and sugar until pale and thick. Add the vanilla and the chocolate mixture and beat until well blended. Add the flour mixture and beat again until well blended. Stir in the pecans, marshmallows, and chopped chocolate (or chocolate chips).

3. Drop the dough by rounded tablespoons, 2 inches apart, onto the prepared baking sheets.

4. Bake for 15 minutes, until shiny and cracked on top. Allow the cookies to cool for 5 minutes on the baking sheet, then carefully transfer to wire racks to finish cooling.

Note: These cookies are fragile when hot, so cooling them for 5 minutes on the baking sheet is important. The sugary ingredients make the cookies very sticky, however, so removing them carefully and promptly (before the sugar hardens completely) with a clean spatula is also important.

• *Makes about 3 dozen cookies*

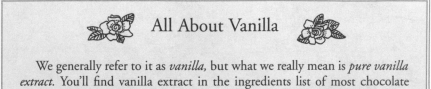

All About Vanilla

We generally refer to it as *vanilla,* but what we really mean is *pure vanilla extract.* You'll find vanilla extract in the ingredients list of most chocolate cookie recipes because, as the Aztecs knew centuries ago, it heightens the delicious taste of chocolate.

The process of cultivating, harvesting, curing, and extracting the flavor from the best vanilla beans is long and arduous, but it yields a superb product. Although some of our pure vanilla extract comes from Tahiti, most is imported from Madagascar. These are the kinds to look for. You'll find them in any good cookware shop or gourmet store, and they're worth every penny. *Don'ts:* Don't buy or use imitation vanilla; it can't compare to the real thing. And don't buy Mexican vanilla extract unless your supplier can guarantee a product unadulterated by a toxic plant derivative called *coumarin.*

Store pure vanilla extract in a cool, dark place for up to 1 year.

My Grandmother's Chocolate Drops

This recipe makes a lot of cookies, but there's a reason for it: My grandmother had four children and they all loved cookies as much as she did. Ten dozen small cookies—crisp on the outside, chewy on the inside—didn't last long in that household.

2 cups flour
2 teaspoons baking powder
½ teaspoon salt
½ cup (1 stick) unsalted butter,
   at room temperature
1¾ cups sugar

1 egg
½ cup milk
1 teaspoon vanilla extract
2 ounces unsweetened chocolate,
   melted and cooled

1. Preheat the oven to 350°F; grease 1 or 2 baking sheets. In a small bowl, stir or whisk together the flour, baking powder, and salt.

2. In a large bowl, cream the butter and sugar. Add the egg, milk, vanilla, and melted chocolate and beat until well blended. Gradually add the flour mixture, blending well after each addition.

3. Drop the dough by rounded teaspoons, 1½ inches apart, onto the prepared baking sheet.

4. Bake for 11 minutes. Let the cookies cool for 1 or 2 minutes on the baking sheet, then transfer to wire racks to finish cooling.

- *Makes about 10 dozen cookies*

Chocolate Snickerdoodles

These cookies are bursting with raisins and nuts. The dough contains nutmeg, too, and the cookies are sprinkled with cinnamon-sugar before they go into the oven.

1½ cups flour
½ teaspoon baking soda
¼ teaspoon salt
½ teaspoon nutmeg
½ cup (1 stick) unsalted butter,
*   at room temperature*
¾ cup sugar

1 egg
2 ounces semisweet chocolate,
*   melted and cooled*
½ cup coarsely chopped walnuts
½ cup dark raisins
2 tablespoons sugar stirred with
*   1½ teaspoons cinnamon*

1. Preheat the oven to 375°F; grease 1 or 2 baking sheets. In a small bowl, stir or whisk together the flour, baking soda, salt, and nutmeg.

2. In a large bowl, cream the butter and sugar. Add the egg and melted chocolate and beat until well blended. Gradually add the flour mixture, blending well after each addition. Stir in the walnuts and raisins.

3. Drop the dough by tablespoons, 1 inch apart, onto the prepared baking sheet. Sprinkle each drop with the sugar-cinnamon mixture, patting it lightly with your fingers to be sure it adheres.

4. Bake for 12 minutes for slightly chewy cookies, 13 minutes for crisper ones. Let the cookies cool for 1 or 2 minutes on the baking sheet, then transfer to wire racks to finish cooling.

• *Makes about 3½ dozen cookies*

Crunchy Peanut Butter–Chocolate Chip Cookies

Thick and crisp and crammed full of peanuts and chocolate chips, with a wonderful peanut butter flavor—these are cookies for peanut-lovers. Great for lunchboxes and after-school snacks.

1¾ cups flour
½ teaspoon baking powder
¼ teaspoon salt
10 tablespoons (1 stick plus 2 tablespoons) unsalted butter, at room temperature
¼ cup sugar
¾ cup packed dark brown sugar

1 egg
1 teaspoon vanilla extract
3 ounces unsweetened chocolate, melted and cooled
¼ cup peanut butter (crunchy or smooth)
¾ cup chopped unsalted peanuts
¾ cup semisweet chocolate chips

1. Preheat the oven to 350°F; grease 1 or 2 baking sheets. In a medium-size bowl, stir or whisk together the flour, baking powder, and salt.

2. In a large bowl, cream the butter, sugar, and brown sugar. Add the egg and vanilla and beat until well blended. Add the melted chocolate and peanut butter and beat again until well blended. Gradually add the flour mixture, blending well after each addition. Stir in the chopped peanuts and chocolate chips. The dough will be rather crumbly.

3. Drop the dough by tablespoons, 2 inches apart, onto the prepared baking sheet. (Because the dough is crumbly, you may have to press it together a bit right on the baking sheet.) With a fork, gently flatten each drop of dough to about ¼ inch thick.

4. Bake for 11 minutes. Let the cookies cool for 1 or 2 minutes on the baking sheet, then transfer to wire racks to finish cooling.

- *Makes about 4 dozen cookies*

Tip from the Cookie Jar

If you don't own any cookie cutters, don't despair: Use a pizza cutter or pastry wheel to cut rolled dough into diamonds, squares, or triangles; use the rim of a glass, dusted with flour, to cut circles; use a small, sharp knife to cut shapes by hand— try hearts, crescents, and stars for starters.

Spiced Chocolate Drop Cookies

If you like spice cake, you'll love these smooth-topped, cakelike little spice cookies. The buttermilk gives them a tender texture, and the brown sugar enhances the spice combination. If you want to dress them up, drizzle them with a little Vanilla Glaze (page 120).

1½ cups flour
1 teaspoon baking powder
½ teaspoon baking soda
½ teaspoon salt
1 teaspoon cinnamon
¼ teaspoon ground cloves
¼ teaspoon nutmeg
½ cup (1 stick) unsalted butter,
  at room temperature

½ cup sugar
½ cup packed light brown sugar
2 eggs
1 teaspoon vanilla extract
3 ounces unsweetened chocolate,
  melted and cooled
½ cup buttermilk

1. Preheat the oven to 350°F; grease and flour 1 or 2 baking sheets. In a small bowl, stir or whisk together the flour, baking powder, baking soda, salt, and spices.

2. In a large bowl, cream the butter, sugar, and brown sugar. Add the eggs, vanilla, and melted chocolate and beat until well blended. Add the flour mixture and the buttermilk alternately, in 3 parts, blending well after each addition.

3. Drop the dough by rounded teaspoons, 1½ inches apart, onto the baking sheet.

4. Bake for 12 minutes. Allow the cookies to cool on the baking sheet for 1 or 2 minutes, then transfer to wire racks to finish cooling. The cooled cookies will have a tender, cakelike texture.

- *Makes about 7 dozen cookies*

Tip from the Cookie Jar

Experiment with sandwiches: Icebox cookies make great sandwich cookies—try a pair of Chocolate-Orange Icebox Cookies filled with Mint Buttercream (page 108) or a pair of Cocoa Crisps with Lemon Cream Filling (page 106). Other delicious filling possibilities: peanut or almond butter; jam or preserves; marmalade; fruit butter; sweetened cream cheese.

Chocolate-Coconut Macaroons

*M*acaroon fans will adore these bite-size chewy cookies with a rich almond flavor. Note that the cookies are made with store-bought pure almond paste—don't try to substitute marzipan or plain ground almonds.

*7 ounces commercial pure almond
  paste* (not *marzipan*)
2 tablespoons flour
Pinch of salt
*2 ounces semisweet chocolate,
  melted and cooled*

3 egg whites
1 tablespoon sugar
½ teaspoon vanilla extract
1 cup sweetened shredded coconut

1. Preheat the oven to 325°F; grease and flour 1 or 2 baking sheets.

2. Break the almond paste into small pieces and place in the bowl of a food processor. Sprinkle with the flour and salt. Add the melted chocolate and process until the mixture looks like very small crumbs or coarse cornmeal. Be sure to scrape down the bowl several times. Do not overprocess or the mixture will become too thick and sticky.

3. In a large bowl, beat the egg whites until foamy. Add the sugar and vanilla and continue beating until the whites stand in firm, glossy, moist peaks. Gradually fold the almond paste mixture into the beaten whites; the whites will deflate quite a bit. Fold in the coconut.

4. Drop the dough by rounded teaspoons, 1 inch apart, onto the prepared baking sheets.

5. Bake for 23 minutes, watching to be sure the edges don't burn. Let the macaroons cool on the baking sheet for 5 minutes. Use a small spatula to transfer to wire racks to finish cooling; don't be surprised if the macaroons stick to the baking sheet a bit.

- *Makes about 4½ dozen cookies*

Triple Chocolate Cookies

*Unsweetened chocolate, cocoa powder, and white chocolate all go into these crisp, delicious drop cookies. **Tip:** When you chop white chocolate, it will break into chips, chunks, and tiny crumbs; for this recipe, use only the chips and chunks.*

1⅓ cups flour
2 tablespoons cocoa powder
¼ teaspoon salt
¾ cup (1½ sticks) unsalted butter,
  at room temperature
⅔ cup sugar

⅓ cup packed light brown sugar
1 egg
1 teaspoon vanilla extract
2 ounces unsweetened chocolate,
  melted and cooled
½ cup chopped white chocolate

1. Preheat the oven to 325°F; grease 1 or 2 baking sheets. In a small bowl, stir or whisk together the flour, cocoa, and salt.

2. In a large bowl, cream the butter, sugar, and brown sugar. Add the egg, vanilla, and melted chocolate and beat until well blended. Gradually add the flour mixture, blending well after each addition. Stir in the chopped white chocolate.

3. Drop the dough by rounded teaspoons, 2 inches apart, onto the prepared baking sheet.

4. Bake for 16 to 17 minutes. Allow the cookies to cool for 5 minutes on the baking sheet, then transfer to wire racks to finish cooling.

· *Makes about 4½ dozen cookies*

Bar Cookies

Next to drop cookies, bar cookies are the simplest to make: Spread the dough evenly in the baking pan (being sure to use the correct size of pan, as specified in the recipe), bake, and cut into squares or rectangles.

Tip: Bar cookies, individually wrapped in plastic, are terrific for lunchboxes or snacks.

Chocolate–Cream Cheese Squares

Oreo cookies are the secret ingredient in these luscious squares; they're used to make the crumb crust, and they're sprinkled on top of the cream cheese filling to make a crisp topping.

For the bottom layer and topping:
- 22 Oreo cookies
- Pinch of salt
- ½ cup finely chopped toasted pecans
- ½ cup (1 stick) unsalted butter or margarine, melted and cooled

For the filling:
- 6 ounces cream cheese, at room temperature
- ½ cup sugar
- 1 egg
- 2 ounces semisweet chocolate, melted and cooled
- ½ teaspoon vanilla extract
- 3 tablespoons flour

1. Preheat the oven to 350°F; grease and flour a 9 x 9-inch baking pan.
2. Make the bottom layer: Break the Oreos (cookies *and* filling) into the bowl of a food processor and process until broken down into fine crumbs. Remove ½ cup crumbs and reserve them for the topping. Add the salt, pecans, and butter to the crumbs remaining in the processor bowl and mix well with a few bursts of power. Pat the mixture evenly into the prepared pan. Bake for 12 minutes. Set aside on a wire rack to cool slightly.
3. Make the filling: In a large bowl, beat the cream cheese and sugar until smooth. Add the egg, melted chocolate, and vanilla and blend well. Add the flour and blend again.

4. Pour the filling over the partially baked bottom layer, tilting the pan to spread it evenly. Sprinkle with the reserved Oreo crumbs.

5. Bake for 25 minutes longer. Let the pan cool completely on a wire rack, then cut into 25 squares (5 squares by 5 squares).

- *Makes 25 squares*

Tip from the Cookie Jar

To dress up icebox cookies, spread finely chopped nuts on waxed. paper and roll the uncut log of cookie dough back and forth to add an even coating of nuts. Be sure the nuts are firmly embedded in the dough. Slice the log and bake the cookies as described in the recipe.

Chocolate-Date Bars

The combination of chocolate, dates, and brown sugar yields moist, cakelike bars with a mellow sweetness. The glaze topping is optional but very attractive.

1¼ cups flour
¾ teaspoon baking soda
¼ teaspoon salt
8 ounces pitted dates, chopped or
  snipped into small pieces
¾ cup packed light brown sugar
3 tablespoons light corn syrup
½ cup (1 stick) unsalted butter

½ cup water
1 cup (5 to 6 ounces) chopped
  semisweet chocolate
2 eggs, beaten
¾ cup milk
1 cup chopped toasted walnuts
Vanilla Glaze (optional; page 120)

1. Preheat the oven to 350°F; grease a 10½ x 15½-inch jelly roll pan. In a small bowl, stir or whisk together the flour, baking soda, and salt.

2. In a large heavy saucepan over medium heat, stir together the dates, brown sugar, corn syrup, butter, and water. Simmer just until the dates are softened and the other ingredients are melted and well combined, about 5 minutes. Transfer the mixture to a large bowl, add the chopped chocolate, and stir until melted. When the mixture is cool, add the beaten eggs and blend well. Add the flour mixture alternately with the milk, in 3 parts, blending well after each addition. Stir in the chopped walnuts.

3. Spread the batter evenly in the prepared pan.

4. Bake for 25 minutes, until a toothpick inserted in the center of the pan comes out clean and the crisp edges have pulled away from the sides of the pan.

Allow the pan to cool completely on a wire rack. If you like, drizzle with Vanilla Glaze before cutting into bars; let the glaze firm up at room temperature or in the refrigerator. Cut into 48 bars (6 bars by 8 bars).

• *Makes 48 bars*

Tip from the Cookie Jar

Here's a super-easy chocolate frosting trick: Sprinkle a few *miniature* chocolate chips on each hot-from-the-oven cookie; let the chips melt for 1 or 2 minutes, then spread with a spatula. Great on bar cookies, too, as in Chocolate-Cherry Squares with Mini-Chip Frosting, page 34. Sprinkle, melt, and spread the chips *before* cutting into bars or squares.

Chocolate-Lemon Bars

~

𝒯ry this marvelous combination of a rich chocolate cookie layer topped with a tangy lemon custard, decorated with chocolate glaze. It's crucial to use fresh lemon juice in this recipe; bottled lemon juice just won't do.

For the bottom layer:

1¼ cups flour
¼ cup cocoa powder, sifted
½ teaspoon baking powder
⅛ teaspoon salt
½ cup (1 stick) unsalted butter,
  at room temperature
½ cup sugar
1 egg
½ teaspoon vanilla extract

For the topping:

2 eggs
¼ cup sugar
Grated zest of 1 large lemon
  (about 2 teaspoons)
1½ tablespoons flour
5 tablespoons strained fresh lemon juice

For the glaze:

2 ounces semisweet chocolate,
  chopped
1 teaspoon neutral vegetable oil
  (corn, safflower, canola, or sunflower)
1 tablespoon water

1. Preheat the oven to 350°F; grease a 9 x 9-inch baking pan.

2. Make the bottom layer: In a small bowl, stir or whisk together the flour, cocoa, baking powder, and salt. In a large bowl, cream the butter and sugar. Add the egg and vanilla and beat until well blended. Gradually add the flour mixture, blending well after each addition.

With a spatula, spread the dough evenly in the prepared pan. Bake for 16 minutes. Place the pan on a wire rack to cool slightly.

3. Make the topping: In a large bowl, beat the eggs and sugar until pale yellow and very thick. Add the grated zest and flour and beat until well blended. Gradually add the lemon juice, beating well after each addition. Pour evenly over the chocolate layer in the pan.

4. Bake for 18 to 22 minutes longer, until the topping is set and the edges are golden brown. Carefully run a sharp knife around the edge of the pan; let the pan cool completely on a wire rack.

5. Make the glaze: In a small heavy saucepan over very low heat, melt the chocolate with the oil and water, stirring constantly until smooth. Drizzle the warm glaze over the topping. Refrigerate the pan to harden the glaze quickly. Use a knife dipped in hot water to cut into 20 bars (5 bars by 4 bars).

- *Makes 20 bars*

Chocolate-Cherry Squares with Mini-Chip Frosting

Here's another great flavor pairing—chocolate and tart-sweet dried cherries. The frosting requires no work at all because it's made with semisweet mini-chips that melt on the hot dough.

¼ pound pitted dried sweet cherries	¼ teaspoon salt
3 ounces unsweetened chocolate, chopped	2 eggs
½ cup (1 stick) unsalted butter	¾ cup flour
1 cup sugar	⅔ cup miniature semisweet
1 teaspoon vanilla extract	chocolate chips

1. Preheat the oven to 325°F; grease and flour a 9 x 9-inch baking pan. Simmer the dried cherries in 1 cup of water in a small saucepan, until softened, 4 to 5 minutes. Drain, pat dry on paper towels, and chop into pea-size pieces.

2. In a small saucepan over low heat, melt the chocolate and the butter, stirring until smooth. Transfer to a large bowl and allow to cool until just warm. Beat in the sugar, vanilla, and salt, then beat in the eggs 1 at a time. Gradually add the flour, blending well after each addition. Stir in the chopped cherries.

3. Spread the batter evenly in the prepared pan.

4. Bake for 30 minutes, until the top is dry and a toothpick inserted in the center of the pan comes out almost clean. Place the pan on a wire rack.

5. Immediately sprinkle the chocolate chips evenly over the hot dough; the chips will soften and melt. Use a small spatula to spread the melted chocolate

evenly. Let the pan cool completely, then cut into 25 squares (5 squares by 5 squares).

• *Makes 25 squares*

Icing for Decorative Piping

This icing dries hard, crisp, and white. If you like, divide it among several bowls and tint each bowl with a small amount of food coloring.

Tip: This recipe may be halved or doubled if necessary.

4½ cups (1 pound) confectioners' sugar, sifted
¾ teaspoon cream of tartar
3 egg whites
½ teaspoon vanilla extract

Stir the ingredients together in a deep bowl. Beat at high speed for 5 minutes, until the icing is firm and holds stiff peaks. Refrigerate, tightly covered with plastic wrap, until ready to use. If the icing softens and loses volume while waiting, bring to room temperature, sift in a spoonful or 2 of confectioners' sugar and a pinch of cream of tartar, and beat at high speed until firm.

• *Makes about 2 cups*

Glazed Coffee Squares

These are bar cookies for grownups—chewy, with a distinct coffee flavor, and glazed with a generous layer of semisweet chocolate. Note that there's no butter in this recipe.

1 cup flour
½ teaspoon baking powder
⅛ teaspoon salt
2 ounces semisweet chocolate, chopped
2 ounces unsweetened chocolate, chopped
1 tablespoon light corn syrup
2 eggs
1 cup sugar
¼ cup neutral vegetable oil (corn, safflower, canola, or sunflower)

1½ teaspoons vanilla extract
1½ tablepoons instant coffee granules dissolved in 2 tablespoons boiling water
½ recipe Semisweet Chocolate Glaze (page 121)
Chocolate-covered coffee beans for decoration (optional)

1. Preheat the oven to 350°F; grease and flour a 9 x 9-inch baking pan. In a small bowl, stir or whisk together the flour, baking powder, and salt. In a heavy saucepan over low heat, melt the semisweet chocolate, unsweetened chocolate, and corn syrup together, stirring until blended and smooth; set aside to cool.

2. In a large bowl, beat the eggs and sugar until pale and thick. Add the oil and vanilla and beat until well blended. Add the chocolate mixture and dissolved coffee and beat again. Gradually add the flour mixture, blending well after each addition.

3. Spread the batter evenly in the prepared pan.

4. Bake for 20 to 23 minutes, until a toothpick inserted in the center of the pan comes out almost clean. Allow to cool on a wire rack, then spread the glaze over the dough. If you like, mark the still-soft glaze into 25 squares (5 squares by 5 squares) and press a chocolate-covered coffee bean in the center of each square. Let the glaze firm up at room temperature or in the refrigerator. Cut into 25 squares (5 squares by 5 squares).

- *Makes 25 squares*

Cookies to Send at Christmas

A gift of homemade cookies is a joy at any time of year, but at Christmas it's especially treasured. Guarantee the success of your gift by choosing appropriate cookies that travel well. If they're just going next door or down the block, feel free to make somewhat more fragile varieties. For friends and relatives far away, choose sturdy cookies and wrap them securely; see page 102 for mailing advice.

Short-distance cookies:

Long-distance cookies:

Crisp Brownie Cookies

These cookies are thinner and crisper than ordinary brownies, but just as delicious—rich and chocolaty with plenty of nuts for crunch. Toasting the nuts is important for the crunchiness, so don't skip that bit of preparation.

¾ cup (1½ sticks) unsalted
   butter, at room temperature
1¼ cups sugar
1 egg

1 teaspoon vanilla extract
3 ounces unsweetened chocolate, melted and cooled
1 cup flour stirred with ⅛ teaspoon salt
1½ cups chopped toasted walnuts or pecans

1. Preheat the oven to 350°F; grease and flour a 10½ x 15½-inch jelly roll pan.

2. In a large bowl, cream the butter and sugar. Add the egg, vanilla, and melted chocolate and beat until well blended. Gradually add the flour, blending well after each addition. Stir in half the chopped nuts.

3. Using a small metal spatula, spread the batter evenly in the prepared pan. Sprinkle the remaining nuts over the batter and use a pancake turner to press them down firmly so they are embedded in the batter.

4. Bake for 20 minutes, until dry and crisp-looking; a finger pressed into the cookies will make a soft dent. Place the pan on a wire rack; immediately run a knife around the edge of the pan, then divide into 50 bars (5 bars by 10 bars) by scoring deeply with a sharp knife or pizza cutter. *Do not remove the cookies yet.* Allow to cool completely on the wire rack, then cut again on the scored lines and carefully remove from the pan.

• *Makes 50 bars*

One-Bowl Fudgies

Fudgies, cut in small squares, will do the trick for any chocolate craving. They are intensely chocolaty and simply delicious. Easy to make, too, in just one bowl.

5 ounces unsweetened chocolate, chopped
½ cup (1 stick) unsalted butter
2 tablespoons light corn syrup
1 cup plus 2 tablespoons sugar
1 teaspoon vanilla extract

½ teaspoon salt
3 eggs
⅔ cup flour
⅔ cup semisweet chocolate chips
  or chopped semisweet chocolate

1. Preheat the oven to 350°F; grease and flour a 9 x 9-inch baking pan.
2. In a large metal bowl set over a saucepan containing 2 inches of barely simmering water, melt the unsweetened chocolate, the butter, and the corn syrup, *whisking* until smooth. Remove the bowl from the saucepan and allow to cool until warm. Whisk in the sugar, vanilla, and salt, then whisk in the eggs 1 at a time. Add the flour and *stir* just until mixed. Stir in the chocolate chips.
3. Spread the batter evenly in the prepared pan.
4. Bake for 25 minutes, until a toothpick inserted in the center of the pan comes out almost clean. Allow to cool completely on a wire rack, then cut into 36 squares (6 squares by 6 squares).

• *Makes 36 small squares*

Diamonds with Vanilla-Hazelnut Topping

Enjoy the wonderful counterpoint of chocolate and vanilla, with a crunch of hazelnuts, in these bars. They are best on the second day, so make them today and eat them tomorrow.

1 cup flour
½ teaspoon baking powder
¼ teaspoon salt
4 ounces unsweetened chocolate, chopped
10 tablespoons (1 stick plus 2 tablespoons) unsalted butter

1 cup sugar
1½ teaspoons vanilla extract
2 eggs
Vanilla Glaze (page 120)
1 cup chopped toasted hazelnuts

1. Preheat the oven to 350°F; grease and flour a 10½ x 15½-inch jelly roll pan. In a small bowl, stir or whisk together the flour, baking powder, and salt.

2. In a heavy saucepan over low heat, melt the chocolate and butter, stirring to combine. Transfer to a large bowl and allow to cool until just warm. Add the sugar and vanilla and beat well. Beat in the eggs 1 at a time. Gradually add the flour mixture, blending well after each addition. The batter will be rather thick and sticky.

3. Spread the batter evenly in the prepared pan.

4. Bake for 15 minutes, until the top is dry and a toothpick inserted in the center comes out clean. Allow to cool completely on a wire rack. Do not cut yet.

5. Spread all the Vanilla Glaze evenly over the dough and sprinkle immediately with the toasted hazelnuts; lightly press the nuts into the glaze. Let the glaze

firm up at room temperature or in the refrigerator. Cut into diamonds as shown. For the best flavor, let the cookies ripen overnight.

• *Makes about 40 diamonds plus 10 smaller pieces*

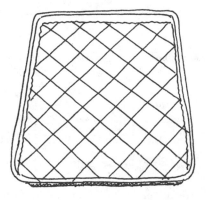

Peanut Brittle–Chocolate Bars

These bar cookies are a cross between brownies and candy. They are thin and crisp, very chocolaty, with bits of peanut candy scattered all the way through. Irresistible.

¾ cup (1½ sticks) unsalted butter,
   at room temperature
¼ cup sugar
1 cup packed light brown sugar
1 egg
1 teaspoon vanilla extract

3 ounces unsweetened chocolate,
   melted and cooled
1 cup flour stirred with
   ⅛ teaspoon salt
1½ cups coarsely chopped Planters Peanut
   Bars (5 bars, each 1.6 ounces)

1. Preheat the oven to 350°F; grease and flour a 10½ x 15½-inch jelly roll pan.

2. In a large bowl, cream the butter, sugar, and brown sugar. Add the egg, vanilla, and melted chocolate and beat until well blended. Gradually add the flour, blending well after each addition. Stir in the chopped peanut bars.

3. Using a small metal spatula, spread the batter evenly in the prepared pan.

4. Bake for 23 to 25 minutes, until a toothpick inserted in the center of the pan comes out almost clean. Take care not to let the edges burn. Place the pan on a wire rack; immediately run a knife around the edge of the pan, then divide into 40 bars (5 bars by 8 bars) by scoring deeply with a sharp knife or pizza cutter. *Do not remove the cookies yet.* Allow to cool completely on the wire rack, then remove the cookies carefully, breaking them apart on the scored lines.

• *Makes 40 bars*

Shaped or Molded Cookies

These cookies are made of dough that is shaped or molded by hand into little balls or crescents, into flat disks, cups, or slender ropes, or even into small loaves that are sliced after baking.

Tip: Shaped or molded cookies containing a high proportion of butter are best made in a cool kitchen with cool hands, and placed on a cool (or chilled) cookie sheet.

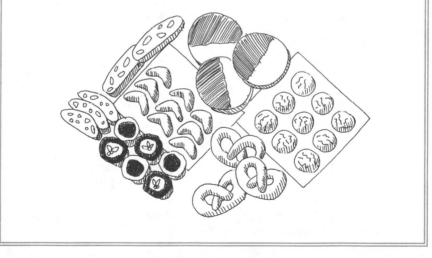

Big Black-and-White Cookies

Old-fashioned black-and-whites from a bakery are big, round vanilla cookies with a cakelike texture, iced with vanilla and chocolate glazes—a half-moon of each glaze tops each cookie. In this updated recipe, the glaze is applied in the same way but the cookie is chocolate.

3 cups flour
1½ teaspoons baking powder
1 teaspoon baking soda
¼ teaspoon salt
3 ounces semisweet chocolate, chopped
½ cup (1 stick) unsalted butter
1 egg
1 egg yolk
1½ cups sugar
¾ cup sour cream

For the chocolate glaze:
1 ounce unsweetened chocolate
2 tablespoons unsalted butter
3 tablespoons heavy cream
½ teaspoon vanilla extract
¾ cup sifted confectioners' sugar

For the vanilla glaze:
1 tablespoon unsalted butter, melted
¾ teaspoon vanilla extract
2 tablespoons milk
Pinch of salt
1¾ cups sifted confectioners' sugar

1. Preheat the oven to 350°F; grease 1 or 2 baking sheets. In a medium-size bowl, stir or whisk together the flour, baking powder, baking soda, and salt. In a medium saucepan over low heat, melt the chocolate and butter, stirring until blended and smooth; allow to cool.

2. In a large bowl, beat the egg, egg yolk, and sugar until thick and pale. Add the sour cream and beat well. Add the flour mixture and the chocolate mixture

alternately, in 4 parts, blending well after each addition. The dough will be thick and sticky. Let the dough rest in the bowl for about 30 minutes, until even thicker but less sticky.

pat out

3. Make several cookies at a time: For each cookie, place ¼ cup of dough on the prepared baking sheet, leaving at least 2½ inches between mounds of dough. (The dough spreads a great deal during baking, so you will be able to fit only 4 or 5 cookies on the baking sheet.) Dust your fingers with flour and pat out each mound of dough to a neat round, 3½ inches in diameter.

4. Bake for 15 minutes. Let the cookies cool on the baking sheet for 5 minutes, then carefully transfer to wire racks to finish cooling. Brush any loose crumbs from the top of the cookies.

5. Make the glazes: For the chocolate glaze, melt the chocolate and butter in a heavy saucepan over low heat, stirring until smooth and blended. Add the remaining ingredients and whisk until smooth. Cover with a piece of plastic wrap pressed directly onto the surface of the glaze.

For the vanilla glaze, stir together the butter, vanilla, milk, and salt. Add the confectioners' sugar and beat with a spoon until smooth. Cover with a piece of plastic wrap pressed directly onto the surface of the glaze.

6. Use a small spatula to spread chocolate glaze on half of each cooled cookie. (If the chocolate glaze thickens, reheat it briefly, stirring until smooth.) Spread vanilla glaze on the other half of each cookie. Set the cookies aside until the glazes are firm.

• *Makes about 18 cookies*

Chocolate Pretzels

These sweet pretzels are lots of fun—dark and very chocolaty, topped with mocha glaze and sprinkled with very finely chopped nuts that resemble coarse salt if you use your imagination. *Tip:* Don't worry about cracks or flaws in the baked dough; the glaze will conceal them.

7 tablespoons cocoa powder	3 tablespoons light corn syrup
2½ cups flour	2 eggs
½ teaspoon baking powder	1½ teaspoons vanilla extract
⅛ teaspoon salt	Mocha Glaze (page 122)
6 tablespoons unsalted butter, at room temperature	Finely chopped walnuts, almonds, or hazelnuts
⅓ cup sugar	

1. Preheat the oven to 350°F; grease 2 baking sheets. In a medium bowl, sift the cocoa over the flour. Add the baking powder and salt and whisk to blend.

2. In a large bowl, cream the butter and sugar. Add the corn syrup, eggs, and vanilla and beat until well blended. Gradually add the flour mixture, beating well after each addition; as the dough gets very stiff, use a wooden spoon to blend in the flour mixture.

3. Divide the dough in half accurately; a kitchen scale works best for this. Wrap 1 half in plastic and set aside for now; divide the other half into 12 equal pieces. Knead 1 piece slightly (to eliminate any dryness), then roll it back and forth on your work surface to make a rope about 10 inches long. (*Note:* Do not dust the surface or your hands with flour.)

Transfer the rope to the prepared baking sheet and form it into a pretzel shape as shown. Repeat with all the pieces and with the other half of the dough, making 12 pretzels on each baking sheet, leaving 1 inch between pretzels.

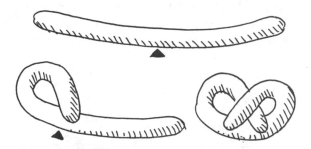

4. Bake each sheet for 9 minutes. Let the pretzels cool for a few minutes on the baking sheet, then transfer carefully to wire racks to finish cooling.

5. Using a small pastry brush, brush the pretzels generously with glaze and sprinkle with chopped nuts while the glaze is still tacky. Set aside on wire racks or waxed paper until the glaze is firm.

- *Makes 2 dozen cookies*

Tender Chocolate-Almond Crescents

A nutty, crumbly dough gives these crescents their melt-in-the-mouth tenderness. Don't omit the sifted confectioners' sugar; the cookies themselves are not very sweet and the confectioners' sugar adds just the right amount of sweetness.

2 cups flour
¾ cup ground blanched almonds
⅛ teaspoon salt
¾ cup (1½ sticks) unsalted butter,
  at room temperature

¼ cup superfine sugar,
  plus extra for shaping
2 ounces semisweet chocolate,
  melted and cooled
Confectioners' sugar for dusting

1. Preheat the oven to 350°F; grease 1 or 2 baking sheets. In a medium-size bowl, stir or whisk together the flour, ground almonds, and salt.

2. In a large bowl, cream the butter and the superfine sugar. Add the melted chocolate and beat until well blended. Gradually add the flour mixture, blending well after each addition. The dough will be crumbly.

3. Form rounded teaspoons of dough into small crescents, pressing the dough firmly into shape. Place the crescents 1 inch apart on the prepared baking sheet.

Tip: At first it may seem difficult to work with this crumbly dough. The warmth of your palms and fingers should be enough to hold the dough together, but you may want to dampen your hands slightly until you master the shaping technique.

4. Bake for 13 minutes. Immediately, while the cookies are still on the baking sheet and still hot, use a fine sieve to sift a generous sprinkling of confectioners' sugar over them. Allow to cool completely either on the baking sheet or on wire racks.

- *Makes about 5½ dozen cookies*

Chocolate Biscotti with Pistachios

Crisp and nutty, the perfect light finish to a good meal, especially with fresh fruit and a glass of wine (or a cup of coffee) in which to dip the biscotti. Note that there is no butter in the biscotti.

4 eggs
1 teaspoon vanilla extract
1¾ cups flour
½ cup cocoa powder, sifted
1 teaspoon baking powder

¼ teaspoon salt
1 cup sugar
1 cup whole shelled unsalted pistachios
½ cup miniature semisweet chocolate chips
2 tablespoons flour

1. Preheat the oven to 325°F; grease 1 baking sheet. For step 5, have ready another baking sheet, ungreased. In a medium-size bowl, whisk or beat together the eggs and vanilla.

2. In a large bowl, whisk together the 1¾ cups flour, cocoa, baking powder, salt, and sugar. Add the egg mixture and stir with a large fork until most of the flour is moistened. Add the pistachios and miniature chocolate chips and mix again; the dough will be stiff and sticky. Sprinkle the 2 tablespoons flour over the dough and work it in as best you can.

3. Divide the dough into 2 equal parts and place on the prepared baking sheet. With well-floured hands, shape each piece into a log about 9 inches long, 3½ inches wide, and ¾ inch high. Leave about 4 inches between the logs on the baking sheet.

4. Bake for 30 minutes. Reduce the oven temperature to 300°. Use a serrated knife to score the top of each log with shallow cuts ½ inch apart, straight across. Let the logs cool on the baking sheet for 10 minutes.

5. On a cutting board, use the serrated knife to cut through each log on the scored lines, making ½-inch-wide slices. Place the slices flat on 2 ungreased baking sheets, ½ inch apart, and bake for 15 minutes at the reduced heat. Turn the slices over and bake for another 15 minutes. Now turn off the oven and leave the biscotti in the warm oven to dry out for a final 15 minutes. Transfer to wire racks and allow to cool completely.

- *Makes about 3 dozen cookies*

Chocolate Mandelbrot

*M*andelbrot—literally, almond bread—are traditional cookies, baked first in small loaves, then sliced into bars and baked again for a crisp texture and nutty flavor. Wonderful at any time of the day, even for breakfast.

3 cups flour
1 teaspoon baking powder
¼ teaspoon salt
¾ cup coarsely chopped blanched almonds
¼ teaspoon ground ginger (optional)

¼ teaspoon cinnamon (optional)
2 ounces semisweet chocolate, chopped
½ cup (1 stick) unsalted butter
3 eggs
¾ cup sugar

1. Preheat the oven to 350°F; grease and flour 1 baking sheet. Have ready another baking sheet, ungreased. In a medium-size bowl, stir or whisk together the flour, baking powder, salt, almonds, and spices. In a small heavy saucepan over low heat, melt the chocolate and butter, stirring until blended and smooth; allow to cool.

2. In a large bowl, beat the eggs and sugar until thick and pale. Add the flour mixture and the chocolate mixture alternately, mixing well with a wooden spoon. The dough will be stiff.

3. Divide the dough into 3 equal parts and place them on the prepared baking sheet. With moistened hands, form each part into a meatloaf shape, 6½ inches long and 2½ inches wide. Be sure there are about 2 inches between loaves on the baking sheet.

4. Bake for 30 minutes. Use a serrated knife to score the top of each log with shallow cuts ½ inch apart, on the diagonal. Let the logs cool on the baking sheet for 10 minutes.

5. On a cutting board, use the serrated knife to cut through each log on the scored lines, making ½-inch-wide slices. Place the slices flat on 2 ungreased baking sheets, ½ inch apart, and bake for 10 minutes. Turn the slices over and bake for another 7 minutes. Transfer to wire racks and allow to cool completely.

- *Makes about 4 dozen cookies*

Double Chocolate–Bourbon Cookies

Here's a dark, rich, and tender cookie, rolled in chopped nuts, with the unmistakable zing of bourbon. This cookie is also great when frozen almost solid—try it.

1 cup flour
3 tablespoons cocoa powder
⅛ teaspoon cinnamon
Pinch of salt
½ cup (1 stick) unsalted butter,
  at room temperature

½ cup packed light brown sugar
¼ cup bourbon
1 egg white, beaten with
  1 tablespoon water
1½ cups very finely chopped pecans
  or walnuts

1. In a small bowl, whisk together the flour, cocoa, cinnamon, and salt.

2. In a large bowl, cream the butter. Gradually add the brown sugar, beating well after each addition. Add the bourbon and beat again. Gradually add the flour mixture, blending well after each addition. Cover the dough and refrigerate for 2 hours. The dough will not become completely firm; it will be sticky but workable.

3. Preheat the oven to 350°F; grease 1 or 2 baking sheets. Dampen your hands and shape the dough into 1-inch balls. (You may have to return the dough to the refrigerator to chill again, especially if your kitchen is very warm.) Roll each ball first in the egg white mixture and then in the chopped nuts. Place the balls 1 inch apart on a greased cookie sheet.

4. Bake for 15 to 20 minutes, until the cookies are still soft but have a light crust. Let the cookies cool on the cookie sheet for about 3 minutes, then transfer to wire racks to finish cooling.

- *Makes about 3 dozen cookies*

Be My Valentine

Sweets for your sweet, sugar for your sugar—it's Valentine's Day, the day of love. Bake a batch of big, crisp, heart-shaped chocolate cookies, spread with vanilla glaze, and let the glaze harden; pipe your love notes right on top.

Rich Chocolate Butter Cookies, page 74, and Chocolate–Sour Cream Sugar Cookies, page 86, are good choices for this project. For the piping, use *Icing for Decorative Piping*, page 35, tinted deep pink; for the how-to, read *Super-Easy, No-Mess Decorative Piping* on page 75.

Chocolate Crackles

Crackles are crisp on the outside, tender and chewy on the inside, with a taste like brownies. The trick for getting that crackled exterior is rolling each cookie in confectioners' sugar before baking.

1½ cups flour	3 ounces unsweetened chocolate,
1½ teaspoons baking powder	melted and cooled
¼ teaspoon salt	2 eggs
6 tablespoons unsalted butter,	1½ teaspoons vanilla extract
at room temperature	Confectioners' sugar
1½ cups sugar	

1. In a small bowl, stir or whisk together the flour, baking powder, and salt.

2. In a large bowl, cream the butter. Add the sugar and melted chocolate and beat until well blended. Add the eggs and vanilla and beat again until well blended. Gradually add the flour mixture, blending well after each addition. Cover and refrigerate the dough for 2 hours, or until firm.

3. Preheat the oven to 350°F; grease 1 or 2 baking sheets. Shape the dough into 1-inch-diameter balls. Dredge each ball in a small bowl of confectioners' sugar to coat it thoroughly. Place the balls 2 inches apart on the prepared baking sheet; the cookies will spread a great deal during baking.

4. Bake for 10 to 12 minutes, watching carefully to be sure the bottoms don't burn. The cookies will be slightly soft in the center when removed from the oven, but they firm up as they cool. Let the cookies cool on the baking sheet for 5 minutes, then transfer to wire racks to finish cooling.

• *Makes about 5 dozen cookies*

Chocolate-Hazelnut Bites

⌒〜⌒

Toasted hazelnuts give these small, elegant cookies their flavor and character. Follow step 3 carefully to be sure the cookies are the right size.

1⅓ cups flour
2 teaspoons baking powder
⅛ teaspoon salt
½ cup (1 stick) unsalted butter,
at room temperature
1 cup sugar

3 egg yolks
2 ounces semisweet chocolate,
melted and cooled
1 cup (¼ pound) skinned hazelnuts,
toasted and finely chopped

(If possible, buy skinned hazelnuts, then toast them according to directions on page 11 and chop them in your food processor)

1. Preheat the oven to 375°F; grease 1 or 2 baking sheets. In a small bowl, stir or whisk together the flour, baking powder, and salt.

2. In a large bowl, cream the butter and sugar. Add the egg yolks and melted chocolate and beat until well blended. Gradually add the flour mixture, blending well after each addition. Stir in the hazelnuts.

3. With moistened hands, shape the dough into ¾-inch-diameter balls. Place the balls 2 inches apart on the prepared baking sheet.

4. Bake for 11 minutes. Let the cookies cool on the baking sheet for 1 or 2 minutes, then transfer to wire racks to finish cooling.

• *Makes about 6½ dozen cookies*

Happy Easter

If you happen to be the Easter Bunny in your house, treat your
family to an Easter basket full of chocolate cookies decorated with
piping.

Make rolled cookies in the shape of rabbits, chicks, eggs, baskets, or bon-
nets. (Rich Chocolate Butter Cookies, page 74, and Chocolate–Sour Cream
Sugar Cookies, page 86, are good choices for this project.) Prepare *Icing for
Decorative Piping,* page 35; leave the icing white or divide it up and tint it
pastel pink, yellow, blue, and green. Pipe designs on the cookies with a pastry bag fitted with a small round tip (#2)—or try the super-
easy piping technique on page 75.

Nestle the cookies on a bed of cellophane grass in
a basket, and add foil-wrapped chocolate eggs and
marshmallow chicks. Tie with pastel ribbons and
trim with 1 or 2 flowers.

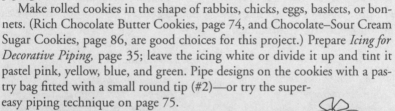

Chocolate Cups I

$\mathcal{T}$reat yourself or your guests to these tiny tartlets with shells made of tender cream cheese dough, filled with creamy chocolate and topped with fancy garnishes. For this recipe you'll need one or two gem muffin pans, which are miniature muffin pans with cups not quite 2 inches across. *Tip:* Be sure to take a look at the following recipe for Chocolate Cups II.

For the cups:
- ½ cup (1 stick) unsalted butter, at room temperature
- 3 ounces cream cheese, softened
- 1 cup flour

For the filling:
- ¼ cup heavy cream
- 2 teaspoons light corn syrup
- 3 ounces semisweet chocolate, chopped
- 1 tablespoon brandy or Grand Marnier

Garnish (choose 1):
slivers of glacé cherries; bits of glacé chestnuts; chopped almonds, macadamia nuts, or hazelnuts; candied violets; tiny mint leaves

1. Make the cups: In a large bowl, cream the butter and cream cheese. Add the flour and blend well. Divide the dough in half (preferably by weight), wrap each half snugly in plastic, and refrigerate for 2 hours, or until firm.

Preheat the oven to 400°F; have ready 1 or 2 gem muffin pans. Work with 1 package of dough at a time: Divide into 12 equal pieces. With floured palms, roll each piece into a ball. Place 1 ball in each cup of the gem pan. With floured fingers, press out the dough to line the bottom and sides of each cup evenly. (The cork from a wine bottle, dusted with flour, also works very well for this.) Use a fork to prick the dough on the bottom of each cup several times.

2. Bake for 10 to 12 minutes, until lightly browned. Let the tartlet shells cool for 5 minutes in the gem pans, then carefully remove them to wire racks to cool completely. The shells are fragile while still warm.

3. Make the filling: Bring the cream and corn syrup to a boil in a small heavy saucepan. Turn off the heat, add the chopped chocolate, and stir until smooth and blended. Stir in the brandy or Grand Marnier. Allow to cool until warm.

4. Fill the cooled shells with about 1 teaspoon of chocolate filling per shell. Top each filled tartlet with your choice of garnish. Refrigerate the tartlets until needed.

- *Makes 2 dozen cups*

Chocolate Cups II

〜 ◦◦ 〜

$\mathscr{C}$hocolate Cups II are the reverse of Chocolate Cups I (page 62): tiny tartlets made of chocolate cream cheese dough, filled with vanilla-flavored whipped cream. For an impressive presentation, make both recipes and arrange the two varieties of tartlets alternately on a tray. To make the cups you'll need one or two gem muffin pans, which are miniature muffin pans with cups not quite 2 inches across.

For the cups:

6 tablespoons unsalted butter,
  at room temperature
3 ounces cream cheese, softened
2 ounces semisweet chocolate,
  melted and cooled
1 cup flour

For the filling:

⅔ cup heavy cream
1 teaspoon vanilla extract
1 tablespoon superfine sugar

Garnish (choose 1):

chocolate or colored sprinkles; chopped dried cranberries, strawberries, or blueberries; small fresh raspberries

1. Make the cups: In a large bowl, beat together the butter, cream cheese, and melted chocolate until light and smooth. Add the flour and blend well. Divide the dough in half (preferably by weight), wrap each half snugly in plastic, and refrigerate for 2 hours, or until firm.

Preheat the oven to 400°F; have ready 1 or 2 gem muffin pans. Work with 1 package of dough at a time: Divide into 12 equal pieces. With floured palms, roll each piece into a ball. Place 1 ball in each cup of the gem pan. With floured fingers, press out the dough to line the bottom and sides of each cup evenly. (The cork from a wine bottle, dusted with flour, also works very well for this.) Use a fork to prick the dough on the bottom of each cup several times.

2. Bake for 10 to 12 minutes, until dry and crisp looking. Let the tartlet shells cool for 5 minutes in the gem pans, then carefully remove them to wire racks to cool completely. The shells are fragile while still warm.

3. Make the filling: In a deep bowl, stir together the cream, vanilla, and sugar. Beat at low speed until the cream is past the soft stage but not quite stiff; do not overbeat.

4. Fill the cooled shells with whipped cream. Top each filled tartlet with your choice of garnish. Refrigerate the tartlets until needed.

- *Makes 2 dozen tarts*

Chocolate Jam Tots

$\mathcal{K}$ids love these traditional cookies, baked with small depressions that are filled with jam, jelly, or marmalade. Wonderful any time of year, but especially good as part of your Christmas cookie assortment.

½ cup (1 stick) unsalted butter,
   at room temperature
¾ cup sugar
¼ teaspoon salt
1 egg
1 egg yolk
1 teaspoon vanilla extract

2 ounces semisweet chocolate,
   melted and cooled
2 cups flour
Apricot or raspberry jam, orange
   marmalade, currant jelly, or other
   favorite preserves

1. In a large bowl, cream the butter and sugar. Add the salt, egg, egg yolk, and vanilla and beat until well blended. Add the melted chocolate and beat again. Gradually add the flour, blending well after each addition. Cover the dough and refrigerate for 2 hours, or until firm.

2. Preheat the oven to 375°F; grease 1 or 2 baking sheets. With moistened hands, shape the dough into 1-inch balls. Place the balls 1½ inches apart on the prepared baking sheet.

3. Bake for 5 minutes. Remove the baking sheet from the oven and use a thimble or a small cork to make a deep depression in the center of each cookie. Return to the oven and bake for 8 minutes if you like chewy cookies, 10 minutes if you prefer crisp ones. Let the cookies cool on the baking sheet for several minutes, then transfer to wire racks to finish cooling.

4. Fill the depressions with your choice of jam, jelly, or marmalade.

• *Makes about 5 dozen cookies*

Fancy Tricks with Glaze: Drizzling or Spreading

Plain cookies (cooled, of course) can be dressed up by drizzling or spreading them with Vanilla Glaze (page 120), Semisweet Chocolate Glaze (page 121), Mocha Glaze (page 122) or Bittersweet Chocolate Glaze (page 123).

Tip: To achieve the right consistency for drizzling, glaze may have to be thinned slightly with water or whatever liquid is used in the recipe.

• Arrange cookies on waxed paper. Fill a sturdy quart-size zip-lock plastic bag with glaze and close the bag securely. Snip a tiny bit off 1 bottom corner, turn the bag so the clipped corner points down, and let the glaze drizzle out onto the cookies—in crisscross lines, spirals, or free-form designs. Allow the glaze to harden before serving.

• Arrange plain cookies close together in rows on waxed paper. Dip a small wire whisk in warm glaze (thinned, if necessary) and then *gently* swing the whisk back and forth a few inches above the cookies, so the glaze drops in threads across the cookies. Work left to right, forward and back, and on the diagonal to vary the direction of the stripes. Let the glaze firm up before serving.

• Use a small spatula to spread unthinned glaze on any flat cookie; use a small pastry brush to spread it on cookies with uneven textures. Set aside on waxed paper until the glaze is firm and dry.

Chocolate Shortbread and Variations

$\mathcal{T}$ender, crisp shortbread, not too sweet, is a universal favorite. The straight chocolate version is great, but you'll want to try the variations, too: Ginger-Chocolate Shortbread; Nut-Chocolate Shortbread; Chocolate–Chocolate Chip Shortbread; Orange-Chocolate Shortbread.

1¾ cups flour	1 cup (2 sticks) butter
½ cup cocoa powder, sifted	½ cup superfine sugar
¼ teaspoon salt	1 teaspoon vanilla extract

1. In a small bowl, stir or whisk together the flour, cocoa, and salt.

2. In a large bowl, cream the butter, sugar, and vanilla. Gradually add the flour mixture, blending well after each addition. If you're making one of the variations, stir in the appropriate ingredients now:

• For Ginger-Chocolate Shortbread, add 5 tablespoons minced crystallized (candied) ginger and 2 teaspoons ground ginger.
• For Nut-Chocolate Shortbread, add ¾ cup finely chopped toasted pecans, almonds, walnuts, or hazelnuts.
• For Chocolate–Chocolate Chip Shortbread, add ½ cup miniature semi-sweet chocolate chips.
• For Orange-Chocolate Shortbread, add 1 tablespoon grated orange zest.

3. Put the dough on an ungreased baking sheet and pat it out to an 8 x 9-inch rectangle. Use the edge of a ruler to score the dough in 1 x 2-inch bars, as

shown. Use a fork to prick each bar 3 or 4 times. Cover tightly with plastic wrap and refrigerate for 1 hour, or until firm.

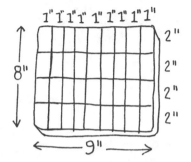

4. Preheat the oven to 325°F; have an additional ungreased baking sheet ready. Cut the chilled dough into bars, following the scored lines, and use a spatula to place them 1 inch apart on the baking sheets.

5. If you have time, bake 1 sheet at a time in the center of the oven for 30 minutes. If you prefer, bake both sheets at the same time, 1 sheet on the middle shelf and 1 on the shelf above, for 20 minutes; then reverse the positions of the 2 baking sheets in the oven for another 10 minutes. Let the bars cool on the baking sheet for 2 or 3 minutes, then carefully transfer to wire racks to finish cooling.

- *Makes 36 bars*

Mocha-Pecan Bites

~⚬~

*B*ecause they really are bite-size, these smooth, tender cookies will disappear fast. Their delicate look and flavor make them an attractive and sophisticated dessert for a dinner party.

2 cups flour
¼ cup cocoa powder, sifted
½ teaspoon baking powder
¼ teaspoon salt
3 ounces semisweet chocolate, chopped
½ cup (1 stick) unsalted butter

2 tablespoons instant coffee granules
1 cup sugar
2 eggs
1 teaspoon vanilla extract
1½ cups finely chopped toasted pecans

1. Preheat the oven to 350°F; grease 1 or 2 baking sheets. In a medium-size bowl, stir or whisk together the flour, cocoa, baking powder, and salt.

2. In a heavy saucepan over low heat, melt the chocolate and butter, stirring until smooth. Turn off the heat and add the instant coffee, stirring until dissolved; let the mixture cool. In a large bowl, beat the sugar, eggs, and vanilla until well blended. Add the cooled chocolate mixture and beat again. Gradually add the flour mixture, blending well after each addition; the dough will be quite stiff. Stir in the pecans.

3. With dampened hands, shape the dough into 1-inch-diameter balls. Place the balls 1½ inches apart on the prepared baking sheet.

4. Bake for 12 minutes, until puffed and dry looking. Transfer the cookies to wire racks to cool.

• *Makes about 6½ dozen cookies*

Chocolate-Rum Bites

It's a snap to make these melt-in-your-mouth, bite-size cookies. Sprinkle generously with confectioners' sugar for an attractive finish.

1½ cups flour
⅓ cup cocoa powder, sifted
⅛ teaspoon salt
1 cup (2 sticks) unsalted butter,
  at room temperature

1 egg yolk
¾ cup confectioners' sugar, sifted
¼ cup light or dark rum
Extra confectioners' sugar for dusting

1. Preheat the oven to 350°F; have ready 1 or 2 baking sheets. In a small bowl, stir or whisk together the flour, cocoa, and salt.

2. In a large bowl, cream the butter until light. Add the yolk, sugar, and rum and beat for 4 minutes. Gradually add the flour mixture, blending well after each addition.

3. With moistened hands, shape the dough into ¾-inch-diameter balls. Place the balls 1 inch apart on the ungreased baking sheet.

4. Bake for 12 minutes. Let the cookies cool on the baking sheet for 1 or 2 minutes, then transfer to wire racks. Using a fine sieve, generously dust the tops of the hot cookies with confectioners' sugar. Allow the cookies to cool completely on the wire racks.

• *Makes about 5½ dozen cookies*

Simple Cookie Decorations

There are several easy ways to decorate your chocolate cookies. The techniques for drizzling with glaze (see page 67) and dipping in glaze (see page 124) are suitable for many cookies. The ideas listed below are most appropriate for the flat cookies in this book—icebox cookies, rolled cookies, most bar cookies, and even a few of the sandwich cookies.

• Mix an egg white with a teaspoon of water; brush mixture on 1 cookie at a time and sprinkle with colored sugar, multicolored nonpareils (tiny dots), or colored (or chocolate) sprinkles.

• Spread glaze (pages 119–123) on 1 cookie at a time. While still tacky, press candies, whole or chopped nuts, miniature chocolate chips, shredded coconut, glacé cherries, etc., into the glaze.

• Spread cookies with Vanilla Glaze (page 120) and allow to set until firm. Using a pastry bag with a small round or star-shaped tip, pipe dots or stars of colored icing (*Icing for Decorative Piping,* page 35) in a random pattern on each cookie.

Rolled Cookies

When you make these perennial favorites, use a rolling pin to roll out the dough (chilled or not, as the recipe specifies) to an even thickness, then cut the rolled dough with cookie cutters or a sharp knife.

Tip: Rolled cookies are especially nice for holidays, when you can make them with holiday cookie cutters—hearts, bunnies, pumpkins, angels, stars, or wreaths.

Rich Chocolate Butter Cookies

*U*se your favorite cookie cutters for this recipe. Serve the cookies unadorned, or decorate with simple piping (see page 79) or a drizzle of glaze (see page 67). Note that the dough does *not* need to be chilled before rolling.

2¼ cups flour
¾ teaspoon baking powder
¼ teaspoon salt
¾ cup (1½ sticks) unsalted butter,
  at room temperature

¾ cup sugar
2 egg yolks
1 teaspoon vanilla extract
2 ounces semisweet chocolate,
  melted and cooled

1. Preheat the oven to 350°F; grease 1 or 2 baking sheets. In a small bowl, stir or whisk together the flour, baking powder, and salt.

2. In a large bowl, cream the butter and sugar. Add the egg yolks and vanilla and beat until well blended. Add the melted chocolate and blend again. Gradually add the flour mixture, blending well after each addition.

3. Divide the dough into 3 pieces; there's no need to chill it. Dust a work surface with flour. With flour-dusted hands, pat out 1 piece of dough to about ¼ inch thick; the dough will be crumbly, so keep patting the edges smooth. Now dust a rolling pin with flour and *roll* the dough to about ⅛ inch thick. Cut with your favorite cookie cutter. Use a large spatula or pancake turner to place the cookies 1 inch apart on the prepared baking sheet. Gather up the excess dough for rerolling.

Repeat this process with the remaining pieces of dough.

4. Bake for 12 minutes. Let the cookies cool on the baking sheet for 1 minute, then transfer carefully to wire racks to finish cooling. A cooled cookie will be crisp.

- *Makes about 3 dozen cookies*
  (cut with a 2½-inch round cookie cutter)

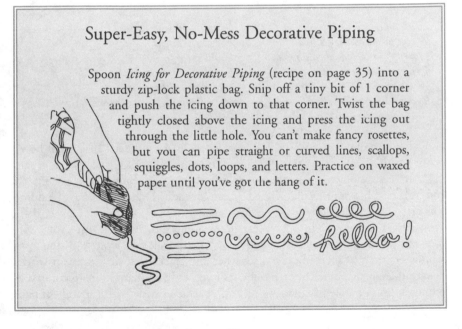

Super-Easy, No-Mess Decorative Piping

Spoon *Icing for Decorative Piping* (recipe on page 35) into a sturdy zip-lock plastic bag. Snip off a tiny bit of 1 corner and push the icing down to that corner. Twist the bag tightly closed above the icing and press the icing out through the little hole. You can't make fancy rosettes, but you can pipe straight or curved lines, scallops, squiggles, dots, loops, and letters. Practice on waxed paper until you've got the hang of it.

Chocolate-Almond Sandies

*S*andies are named for the sugar topping that gives them a sandy look. To make these big, diamond-shaped cookies, use a diamond-shaped cookie cutter, 3½ inches long, or cut the dough with a sharp knife. Note that this dough does *not* have to be chilled before rolling.

1 cup flour
½ cup cocoa powder, sifted
¾ cup ground blanched almonds
1 teaspoon baking powder
½ teaspoon salt
½ cup (1 stick) unsalted butter,
  at room temperature

1 cup sugar
2 eggs, separated
1 tablespoon milk
1 tablespoon sugar mixed
  with ¼ teaspoon nutmeg
30 or more blanched almond halves

1. Preheat the oven to 375°F; grease 1 or 2 baking sheets. In a small bowl, stir or whisk together the flour, cocoa, ground almonds, baking powder, and salt.

2. In a large bowl, cream the butter and the cup of sugar. Add the egg *yolks* and milk and beat until well blended. Gradually add the flour mixture, blending well after each addition.

3. Divide the dough into 2 pieces; there's no need to chill it. Dust a work surface and rolling pin generously with flour. Gently roll out 1 piece of dough to a little less than ¼ inch thick; pat together any cracks that develop. Cut with a diamond-shaped cookie cutter, 3½ inches long, or use a sharp knife to cut in diamonds approximately 3½ inches long and 2½ inches wide. Use a spatula or pan-

cake turner to place the cookies 1½ inches apart on the prepared baking sheet; the cookies will spread as they bake. Gather up the excess dough for rerolling.

Repeat this process with the second piece of dough.

4. Add a tablespoon of water to the egg whites and whisk just until foamy. Brush the tops of the cookies with egg white and sprinkle with a little of the sugar-nutmeg mixture. Press an almond half in the center of each cookie.

5. Bake for 11 to 13 minutes; the cooled cookies will be crisp. Let the cookies cool on the baking sheet for 1 or 2 minutes, then transfer to wire racks to finish cooling.

• *Makes about 2½ dozen cookies*

Chocolate Biscuits

*H*ere's a recipe for cookies in the English style—tender, not too sweet, and perfect with afternoon tea. To make these, you'll need a scalloped round cookie cutter 2½ inches in diameter, or a similar cookie cutter about the same size.

3½ cups flour
1½ teaspoons baking powder
1 teaspoon baking soda
¼ teaspoon salt
3 ounces semisweet chocolate, chopped
½ cup (1 stick) unsalted butter

2 eggs
1 cup sugar
¾ cup sour cream
1 egg white whisked
  with 1 tablespoon water
Sugar for sprinkling

1. In a medium-size bowl, stir or whisk together the flour, baking powder, baking soda, and salt. In a medium saucepan over low heat, melt the chocolate and butter, stirring until blended and smooth; allow to cool.

2. In a large bowl, beat the 2 whole eggs and sugar until thick and pale. Add the sour cream and beat well. Add the flour mixture and the chocolate mixture alternately, in 4 parts, blending well after each addition. The dough will be thick and sticky. Divide the dough into 3 pieces, wrap each in plastic, and refrigerate for 2 hours, or until firm enough to roll.

3. Preheat the oven to 350°F; grease 1 or 2 baking sheets. Generously dust a work surface and rolling pin with flour. Roll out 1 piece of dough to a little less than ¼ inch thick. Cut with a scalloped round cookie cutter, 2½ inches in diameter. Use a spatula or pancake turner to place the cookies 1 inch apart on the

prepared baking sheet. Brush the top of each cookie with egg white mixture and sprinkle with sugar. Gather up the excess dough for rerolling.

Repeat this process with the remaining pieces of dough.

4. Bake for 11 minutes. Carefully transfer the cookies to wire racks to cool.

- *Makes about 5 dozen cookies*

Simple Piped Designs

Using *Icing for Decorative Piping* (page 35) and either a pastry bag fitted with a small round tip (#2 is a good choice) or a plastic zip-lock bag with a corner snipped off as explained on page 75, try piping some of these simple designs on any flat cookies. Many of the icebox cookies (pages 89 to 101) and rolled cookies (pages 73 to 87) are suitable for piped designs.

Big Chocolate Cookies with Decorations

~~~

This is a great project for a birthday party—prepare a batch of these oversize chocolate cookies for the kids to decorate with chocolate chips, nuts, small candies, colored sugar or sprinkles, raisins, and more. You'll need a round cookie cutter 4 inches in diameter.

2½ cups flour
1 teaspoon baking powder
½ teaspoon salt
½ cup (1 stick) unsalted butter,
   at room temperature
1½ cups sugar

1 egg
1 teaspoon vanilla extract
2½ ounces unsweetened chocolate,
   melted and cooled
¼ cup milk
1 egg white

Decorations (your choice or optional):

Chocolate chips; M&M's, gumdrops, cinnamon redhots or other small candies; colored sprinkles, dots, or sugar; whole or chopped nuts; slivered or halved almonds; dark or light raisins; candied cherries or other candied fruit

1. In a small bowl, stir or whisk together the flour, baking powder, and salt.
2. In a large bowl, cream the butter and sugar. Add the egg, vanilla, and melted chocolate and beat until well blended. Add the flour mixture alternately with the milk, in 3 parts, blending well after each addition. Divide the dough in half, wrap each piece snugly in plastic, and refrigerate for 2 hours, or until firm enough to roll.

3. Preheat the oven to 350°F; grease 1 or 2 baking sheets. Dust your work surface and rolling pin with flour. Roll out 1 piece of dough to a little less than ¼ inch thick. Cut with a round cookie cutter 4 inches in diameter, saving the excess dough for rerolling. Use a pancake turner to place the cookies 1 inch apart on the prepared baking sheet.

Repeat the process with the remaining piece of dough.

4. Whisk the egg white with 1 tablespoon of water. Brush the top of each big cookie with egg white mixture; decorate while the egg white is still damp. Sugars, dots, or sprinkles can be scattered on the damp egg white; nuts, candies, and fruits should be pressed gently but firmly into the dough.

5. Bake for 14 minutes, until the tops look dry and the edges are somewhat cracked. Let the cookies cool on the baking sheet for 2 minutes, then carefully loosen with a pancake turner. Let the cookies cool for 3 minutes longer on the baking sheet. Transfer to wire racks to finish cooling.

- *Makes about 16 cookies*

Chocolate Ravioli

~~~~~~

*L*ike ravioli, each of these cookies is a little pillow stuffed with a tasty filling—but in this case the pillow's not pasta, it's delicious chocolate dough, and the filling is your choice of raspberry jam or chocolate chips, which melt during baking.

2 cups flour
½ cup cocoa powder, sifted
¼ teaspoon baking soda
⅛ teaspoon salt
1 cup (2 sticks) unsalted butter,
  at room temperature

¾ cup sugar
1 egg
1½ teaspoons vanilla extract
Raspberry preserves
Miniature semisweet chocolate chips

1. In a medium-size bowl, stir or whisk together the flour, cocoa, baking soda, and salt.

2. In a large bowl, cream the butter and sugar. Add the egg and vanilla and beat until well blended. Gradually add the flour mixture, blending well after each addition. Divide the dough in half, wrap each piece snugly in plastic, and refrigerate for 1 hour.

3. Preheat the oven to 350°F; grease 1 or 2 baking sheets. Dust your work surface and rolling pin with flour. Roll out 1 piece of dough to an approximate square, ⅛ inch thick. Measure and cut carefully into 1½-inch squares. Place the squares 1 inch apart on the prepared baking sheet. Place a scant ½ teaspoon of raspberry preserves or a teaspoon of miniature chocolate chips in the center of each square. Set aside.

4. Roll out and cut the second piece of dough into 1½-inch squares as described above. Center each new square over one of the filled squares on the baking sheet. Seal each ravioli by pressing the edges together with the tines of a fork, then pierce the top of each ravioli twice with the points of the fork. (*Tip:* If the tines get sticky, dip them in flour.)

Leftover dough can be rolled out and cut into an even number of squares, then made into ravioli as described above.

5. Bake for 14 minutes. Let the cookies cool on the baking sheet for 2 to 3 minutes, then transfer to wire racks to finish cooling.

- *Makes about 4 dozen cookies*

Zebras

~~~

Zebras are beautifully striped cookies, made with basic chocolate and vanilla doughs that are rolled, layered, rolled again, and sliced. Please note that making this cookie requires a bit of experience with rolled dough.

*1 cup (2 sticks) unsalted butter,
  at room temperature*
1 cup sugar
1 teaspoon vanilla extract

⅛ teaspoon salt
2 cups flour
2 tablespoons cocoa powder, sifted

1. In a large bowl, cream the butter, sugar, vanilla, and salt. Gradually add the flour, blending well after each addition. Put half the vanilla dough in another bowl and blend the cocoa into it to make a chocolate dough. Wrap each dough snugly in plastic and refrigerate for about an hour, until chilled but still pliable.

2. Dust your work surface and rolling pin with flour. Roll out or pat each piece of dough to a 6-inch square. Lightly brush the top of the vanilla square with water and cover with the chocolate square; pat the edges flat and square. Dust the top (chocolate) with flour and roll out to a 9-inch square. Cut into 2 equal rectangles; brush the top of 1 with water and cover with the second as shown in the diagram.

3. Now roll out this rectangle to 5 inches wide, keeping the edges square. Cut into 2 long rectangles (each 2½ inches wide), brush the top of 1 with water, and cover with the second. Pat the edges flat and square. Carefully wrap in plastic, place on a baking sheet or flat plate, and refrigerate for 30 minutes.

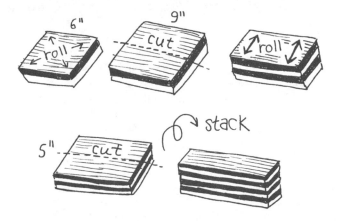

4. Preheat the oven to 350°F; grease 1 or 2 baking sheets. With a sharp knife, cut the layered dough crosswise into striped slices a little less than ¼ inch thick. Place the slices 1½ inches apart on the prepared baking sheet.

Note: This yields rather large cookies. If you prefer daintier cookies, cut each slice in half crosswise to make 2 smaller rectangles. Arrange them 1½ inches apart on the baking sheet.

5. Bake for 12 minutes, until the vanilla dough is just golden. Allow the cookies to cool for 1 or 2 minutes on the baking sheet, then transfer to wire racks to finish cooling.

• *Makes about 3 dozen large cookies*

Chocolate–Sour Cream Sugar Cookies

Thin, crisp rolled cookies to cut into your favorite cookie cutter shapes—animals, crescents, Christmas trees and angels, hearts for Valentine's Day. A scalloped round cookie cutter, 3 inches in diameter, is a good choice, too.

3 cups flour
1 teaspoon baking powder
½ teaspoon baking soda
¼ teaspoon salt
½ cup (1 stick) unsalted butter,
    at room temperature

1¼ cups sugar
1 egg
3 ounces semisweet chocolate,
    melted and cooled
½ cup sour cream

1. In a small bowl, stir or whisk together the flour, baking powder, baking soda, and salt.

2. In a large bowl, cream the butter and sugar. Add the egg and melted chocolate and beat until well blended. Add the flour mixture and the sour cream alternately, in 3 parts, blending well after each addition. Divide the dough into 3 pieces, wrap each in plastic, and refrigerate for 2 hours, or until firm enough to roll.

3. Preheat the oven to 375°F; grease 1 or 2 baking sheets. Dust a work surface and rolling pin with flour. Roll out 1 piece of dough to ⅛ inch thick. Cut with your choice of cookie cutters. Use a spatula or pancake turner to place the cookies 1 inch apart on the prepared baking sheet. Gather up the excess dough for rerolling.

Repeat this process with the remaining pieces of dough.

4. Bake for 12 minutes. Let the cookies cool on the baking sheet for about 1 minute, then transfer to wire racks to finish cooling. A cooled cookie will be crisp.

- *Makes about 4 dozen cookies*

Cookie Storage

Basics: Keep cookies with strong flavors (such as spice or peanut butter) in separate containers so the flavors don't mix. Never store soft cookies and crisp cookies in the same container. *Tip:* Cookies that become a little too soft can be crisped or freshened by heating them in a 325°F oven for 1 or 2 minutes.

Containers: Cookie jars, glass jars, or plastic containers with close-fitting lids are excellent for protecting your cookies and keeping them fresh. So are zip-lock plastic bags, although cookies in plastic bags may, of course, break or crumble.

Freezing: Most cookies freeze well in zip-lock bags or in airtight plastic containers. Bar cookies should be wrapped snugly in plastic wrap (in packets of 4, 8, or any other family-friendly amount), then sealed in zip-lock bags or plastic containers. To defrost, spread cookies in a single layer on a wire rack and let them come to room temperature. If necessary, crisp the cookies in a 325°F oven for 1 or 2 minutes; let them cool before serving.

Cookies for Bake Sales and Bazaars

For most bake sales and bazaars, opt for recipes that use affordable ingredients, are easy to make, yield a lot of cookies, and keep well. Efficiency and speed are important when making large batches, so drop, bar, and icebox cookies are all good choices. These homey styles are irresistible to many patrons, but keep in mind that fancier cookies can be best sellers, too—and you can charge more money for them. So consider including rolled, molded, and sandwich cookies in your selection.

Here are some possibilities:

Icebox Cookies

~ ⌒ ~

*I*cebox cookies (or refrigerator cookies, if you're feeling modern) are sliced from a thoroughly chilled log of dough, then baked like any other cookies. It's important to make the logs as round and smooth as you can, in order to yield a nice round cookie. Use the plastic wrapper to help you achieve this; during the chilling period, remove the log from the refrigerator two or three times and roll it back and forth to keep the cylindrical shape intact.

Tip: Keep a log stashed in the freezer and pull it out any time you crave fresh homemade cookies.

Chocolate-Orange Icebox Cookies

~~~~~

The combination of chocolate and orange is an elegant and sophisticated flavor, and these cookies are terrific for company dinners and parties. Shape the dough into two logs—one to bake now and one to bake on another day, with a yield of about 3½ dozen cookies per log.

2½ cups flour
½ teaspoon baking soda
½ teaspoon salt
1 cup (2 sticks) unsalted butter,
   at room temperature
½ cup sugar
½ cup packed light brown sugar

1 egg
1 teaspoon vanilla extract
2 tablespoons frozen orange juice
   concentrate, thawed
1 tablespoon grated orange zest
2 ounces unsweetened chocolate,
   melted and cooled

1. In a small bowl, stir or whisk together the flour, baking soda, and salt.

2. In a large bowl, cream the butter, sugar, and brown sugar. Add the egg, vanilla, orange juice concentrate, and grated zest and beat until well blended. Add the chocolate and blend again. Gradually add the flour mixture, blending well after each addition. Cover the dough with plastic and refrigerate for 30 minutes to an hour, until chilled but still pliable.

3. Divide the dough in half and place each half on a piece of plastic wrap. Using the plastic to help, shape each half into a smooth log about 2 inches in diameter. Wrap snugly in the plastic and refrigerate for several hours, until very firm, turning and smoothing the logs occasionally.

4. Preheat the oven to 400°F; grease 1 or 2 baking sheets. Unwrap 1 log of dough and use a sharp knife to cut it into ⅛-inch-thick slices. Place the slices ½ inch apart on the prepared baking sheet. Repeat with the second log or reserve it for future use.

5. Bake for 7 minutes, until a cooled cookie is crisp. Let the cookies cool for 1 or 2 minutes on the baking sheet, then transfer to wire racks to finish cooling.

• *Makes about 7 dozen cookies*

Chocolate-Nut Slices

Crisp and scrumptious, easy to prepare, and all too easy to eat. Make the whole recipe or bake only half the dough at a time, keeping the second half for another day.

2¼ cups flour
1½ teaspoons baking powder
¼ teaspoon salt
¾ cup finely chopped toasted pecans
  or walnuts
½ cup (1 stick) unsalted butter,
  at room temperature

1 cup sugar
1 egg
2 tablespoons milk
1 teaspoon vanilla extract
2 ounces unsweetened chocolate,
  melted and cooled

1. In a small bowl, stir or whisk together the flour, baking powder, salt, and chopped nuts.

2. In a large bowl, cream the butter and sugar. Add the egg, milk, vanilla, and melted chocolate and beat until well blended. Gradually add the flour mixture, blending well after each addition.

3. Divide the dough in half and place each half on a piece of plastic wrap. Using the plastic wrap to help, shape each half into a smooth log about 2 inches in diameter. Wrap snugly in the plastic and refrigerate for several hours, until firm, turning and smoothing the logs occasionally.

4. Preheat the oven to 400°F; grease and flour 1 or 2 baking sheets. Unwrap 1 log of dough and use a sharp knife to cut it into ⅛-inch-thick slices. Place the

slices ½ inch apart on the prepared baking sheet. Repeat with the second log or reserve it for future use.

5. Bake for 8 minutes, taking care not to let the cookies burn; they will be slightly soft in the center when removed from the oven. Let the cookies cool for 1 or 2 minutes on the baking sheet, then transfer to wire racks to finish cooling.

- *Makes about 6 dozen cookies*

Cocoa Crisps

These simple cookies have a deep, dark chocolate taste, thanks to the generous amount of cocoa used to make the dough. Use high-quality cocoa for really special cookies.

1¼ cups flour
¾ cup sifted *cocoa powder*
1½ teaspoons baking powder
¼ teaspoon salt

¾ cup (1½ sticks) unsalted butter,
    at room temperature
1¼ cups sugar
1 egg

1. In a medium-size bowl, stir or whisk together the flour, cocoa, baking powder, and salt; be sure the cocoa is evenly distributed in the mixture.

2. In a large bowl, cream the butter and sugar. Add the egg and beat well. Gradually add the flour mixture, blending well after each addition; the dough will be quite soft.

3. Divide the dough in half and place each half on a piece of plastic wrap. Use the plastic to help shape each half into a smooth log about 2 inches in diameter. Wrap snugly in the plastic and refrigerate for several hours, until very firm, turning and smoothing the logs occasionally.

4. Preheat the oven to 400°F; grease 1 or 2 baking sheets. Unwrap 1 log of dough and use a sharp knife to cut it into ⅛-inch-thick slices. Place the slices 1 inch apart on the prepared baking sheet. If the dough becomes soft, refrigerate again until firm.

Repeat with the second log or reserve it for future use.

5. Bake for 7 minutes, making sure the edges of the cookies don't burn. Let the cookies cool for no more than 2 minutes on the baking sheet, then transfer to wire racks to finish cooling.

- *Makes about 5½ dozen cookies*

Cookies to Serve at Christmas

Offering cookies to your holiday guests is a time-honored tradition. Simple delicious cookies are always appreciated, but you may also want to try your hand at a couple of the fancier types.

Simple cookies:

Fancier cookies:

Half-Moon Chocolate Wafers

These are fun: Half of each chocolate cookie is spread with vanilla glaze, like a half moon. Makes an exceptionally pretty presentation for a party.

2½ cups flour
¾ teaspoon baking powder
½ teaspoon salt
¾ cup (1½ sticks) unsalted butter,
   at room temperature
¾ cup sugar
1 egg
4½ tablespoons milk
2 ounces unsweetened chocolate,
   melted and cooled

For the glaze:
   2 cups confectioners' sugar, sifted
   6 tablespoons heavy cream
   2 teaspoons vanilla extract
   Pinch of salt

1. In a medium-size bowl, stir or whisk together the flour, baking powder, and salt.

2. In a large bowl, cream the butter and sugar. Add the egg, milk, and melted chocolate and beat until well blended. Gradually add the flour mixture, blending well after each addition.

3. Divide the dough in half and place each half on a piece of plastic wrap. Using the plastic to help, form each half into a smooth log about 2 inches in diameter. Wrap snugly in the plastic and refrigerate for several hours, until very firm, turning and smoothing the logs occasionally.

4. Preheat the oven to 400°F; grease and flour 1 or 2 baking sheets. Unwrap 1 log of dough and use a sharp knife to cut it into ⅛-inch-thick slices. Place the slices ½ inch apart on the prepared baking sheet. Repeat with the second log or reserve it for future use.

5. Bake for 8 minutes, making sure the cookies don't burn. Let the cookies cool for 1 or 2 minutes on the baking sheet, then transfer to wire racks to finish cooling.

6. Make the glaze: Stir together the confectioners' sugar and the cream. Add the vanilla and salt and beat until smooth. The glaze should be rather thick. Use the glaze right away or cover it with a piece of plastic wrap placed directly on the surface. Spread glaze on half of each cookie. Set aside until the glaze is firm, or refrigerate to speed up the process.

- *Makes about 6½ dozen cookies*

Vanilla and Chocolate Pinwheels

Pinwheel cookies are made with two colors of dough, one placed on top of the other, rolled tightly like a jelly roll, then sliced to reveal two contrasting spirals. These crisp, buttery cookies are truly festive, great for the holidays.

1¾ cups flour
1½ teaspoons baking powder
⅛ teaspoon salt
½ cup (1 stick) unsalted butter,
    at room temperature
1 cup sugar

1 egg yolk
3 tablespoons milk
1 teaspoon vanilla extract
2 ounces unsweetened chocolate,
    melted and cooled

1. In a small bowl, stir or whisk together the flour, baking powder, and salt.

2. In a large bowl, cream the butter and sugar. Add the egg yolk, milk, and vanilla and beat until well blended. Gradually add the flour mixture, blending well after each addition. Put half of this vanilla dough into another bowl and blend in the melted chocolate to make a chocolate dough.

3. Spread a 16-inch-long piece of plastic wrap on your work surface and sprinkle with flour. On the plastic wrap pat out the vanilla dough to a rectangle 12 inches long and 7 inches wide, about ⅛ inch thick. Place the chocolate dough on the vanilla dough and pat it out carefully to cover the vanilla dough. Now pat out the 2 doughs together to a rectangle 13½ inches long and 8½ inches wide.

Using the plastic wrap to help you, roll the 2 doughs tightly together from the long side, as if you were rolling up a jelly roll. Wrap this long log of 2-colored dough snugly in the plastic and refrigerate on a baking sheet for several hours, until very firm, turning and smoothing the log occasionally.

4. Preheat the oven to 350°F; grease 1 or 2 baking sheets. Unwrap the dough and use a sharp knife to cut the roll into ⅛-inch-thick slices. Place the slices ½ inch apart on the prepared baking sheet.

5. Bake for 9 to 10 minutes, until the vanilla dough is just beginning to turn golden. Transfer carefully to wire racks to cool.

- *Makes about 4½ dozen cookies*

The Mailing Game:
Safe Passage for Your Cookies

There's no guarantee that the chocolate cookies you mail will arrive at your aunt's house in the same shape they left yours, but if you follow a few simple rules you'll increase the chance of success.

First, choose appropriate cookies—nothing fragile or brittle, nothing with frosting or moist filling. Soft cookies, bars, drop cookies, and firm cookies all mail well. The list on page 38 will give you a few ideas.

Second, pick a sturdy container with a tight-fitting lid: stiff cardboard box, plastic kitchen container or storage container, cookie tin.

Third, line the container with plastic wrap to protect the cookies from absorbing unwanted odors. (You don't want your cookies to come out of the box tasting faintly of cardboard.) Add a ½-inch layer of slightly crumpled waxed paper to the bottom of the container.

Fourth, make alternating layers of cookies and slightly crumpled waxed paper. (*Important:* If you want to mail crisp cookies in the same package with soft cookies, wrap them separately in plastic so they don't absorb moisture and become soggy. Also, wrap different *varieties* of cookies separately so their flavors don't mingle.) Finish off with another ½-inch layer of crumpled waxed paper. Add the lid—it should sit snugly on the cookies, but not so snugly that it crushes the cookies. Now, if you like, gift-wrap the container.

Finally, if the container is strong enough, simply wrap it in 2 layers of heavy paper and tape it securely. If the container is not very strong, line a larger box with plenty of crumpled newspaper and place the cookie container inside; tuck crumpled newspaper all around the containers. Be sure the container is "floating" in crumpled newspaper. Top with another layer of crumpled newspaper and tape the bigger box closed.

Sandwich Cookies

*H*omemade sandwich cookies are great fun to make and eat. Just bake the cookies, spread half of them with creamy filling, and top with the remaining half. The filling goes between the *wrong* sides of each pair of cookies; be sure to brush any loose crumbs away from the wrong sides before trying to spread the filling.

Tip: If you like, mix and match the fillings. For example, instead of filling the Devil's Food Sandwiches on page 106 with Lemon Cream as in the recipe, substitute the Mint Buttercream that goes with the sandwiches on page 108.

Chocolate-Marshmallow Sandwiches

To make each delectably gooey sandwich, put marshmallow fluff between a pair of thin cookies, then seal the circumference of the sandwich with chocolate glaze so the filling can't escape. If you like, chill the sandwiches so the glaze is firm and crisp.

For the sandwich cookies:

½ cup (1 stick) unsalted butter,
at room temperature
½ cup sugar
1 egg
1½ teaspoons vanilla extract
1 ounce unsweetened chocolate,
   melted and cooled
1½ cups flour stirred
   with ¼ teaspoon salt
1 cup marshmallow fluff (use any
   good commercial variety)

For the glaze:

2 tablespoons unsalted butter
2 ounces unsweetened chocolate
2 tablespoons milk
3 tablespoons water
1¾ cup confectioners' sugar, sifted
1 teaspoon vanilla extract

1. Make the cookies: In a large bowl, cream the butter and sugar. Add the egg, vanilla, and melted chocolate and beat until well blended. Gradually add the flour, blending well after each addition.

2. Divide the dough in half and place each half on a piece of plastic wrap. Using the plastic wrap to help, shape each half into a log 1½ inches in diameter.

Wrap snugly in the plastic and refrigerate for several hours, until very firm, turning and smoothing the logs occasionally.

3. Preheat the oven to 400°F; grease 1 or 2 baking sheets. Unwrap 1 log of dough at a time and use a sharp knife to cut an even number of slices a little more than ⅛ inch thick. Place the slices 1 inch apart on the baking sheet.

4. Bake for 8 minutes; be sure the edges and bottoms don't burn. Let the cookies cool for only 1 minute on the baking sheet, then transfer to wire racks to finish cooling. Brush away any loose crumbs from the cookies.

5. Make the sandwiches: To make 1 sandwich, put a generously rounded teaspoon of marshmallow fluff on the flat side of 1 cookie and cover with the flat side of another cookie. Press together gently, to spread the filling just to the edges of the cookies. Refrigerate all the sandwiches for 10 minutes.

6. Make the glaze: In a medium-sized heavy saucepan over very low heat, stir together the butter, chocolate, milk, and water until smooth and blended. Gradually whisk in the confectioners' sugar, blending until very smooth. Blend in the vanilla. The glaze should still be warm.

7. Roll the *edge* of each sandwich in *warm* glaze, turning the sandwich like a wheel. Be generous with the glaze. Place the sandwiches on a wire rack; the glaze will harden almost immediately, holding the filling securely inside. If necessary, reheat the glaze and stir in a few drops of water to maintain the consistency that is optimum for coating the edges of the sandwiches.

- *Makes about 2 dozen sandwiches*

Devil's Food Sandwiches with Lemon Cream Filling

The crisp cookies for these sandwiches are made by a simple technique of shaping the dough into balls and flattening them with the bottom of a glass. Fill with sensational lemon cream.

For the cookies:

- 2½ cups flour
- ½ cup cocoa powder, sifted
- 1½ teaspoons baking powder
- ½ teaspoon salt
- 1 cup (2 sticks) unsalted butter, at room temperature
- 1½ cups sugar
- 2 eggs
- 2 teaspoons vanilla extract

For the filling:

- ¼ cup (½ stick) unsalted butter, at room temperature
- Grated rind of 1 lemon
- 1 tablespoon fresh lemon juice
- 2 tablespoons sour cream
- 2½ cups confectioners' sugar, sifted

1. Make the cookies: In a small bowl, stir or whisk together the flour, cocoa, baking powder, and salt. In a large bowl, cream the butter and sugar. Add the eggs and vanilla and beat until well blended. Gradually add the flour mixture, blending well after each addition.

2. Divide the dough into 4 parts, wrap each part snugly in plastic, and refrigerate for 1 hour, or until firm.

3. Preheat the oven to 400°F; grease 1 or 2 baking sheets. Have ready a glass with a flat bottom. Unwrap 1 package of dough at a time. Break off pieces of

dough and, with dampened palms, shape into balls about 1 inch in diameter. Place the balls 2 inches apart on the prepared baking sheet. Dust the bottom of the glass generously with flour and use it to flatten each ball to a little less than ¼ inch thick.

4. Bake for 8 minutes, watching carefully to be sure the bottoms of the cookies don't burn. Transfer immediately to wire racks to cool. Brush any loose crumbs from the flat sides of the cooled cookies.

5. Make the filling: In a large bowl, stir all the filling ingredients together, then beat until smooth and spreadable.

6. Make the sandwiches: Turn half the cookies flat side up; divide the filling equally among them and use a small spatula to spread the filling evenly. Top with the remaining cookies, flat side down. Press the sandwiches lightly so they hold together. Unless you're eating them in the next couple of hours, these should be refrigerated.

• *Makes about 4 dozen sandwiches*

Chocolate Sandwiches with Mint Buttercream Filling

~

If you like the combination of mint and chocolate, you'll love these sandwiches. The lightly minted filling has a crunchy surprise—miniature chocolate chips.

For the cookies:

1½ cups flour
½ teaspoon baking powder
¼ teaspoon salt
½ cup (1 stick) unsalted butter,
  at room temperature
½ cup sugar
1 egg yolk
1 teaspoon vanilla extract
3 tablespoons milk
2 ounces unsweetened chocolate,
  melted and cooled

For the filling:

¼ cup (½ stick) unsalted butter,
  at room temperature
1¾ cups confectioners' sugar, sifted
Pinch of salt
¼ teaspoon peppermint extract
⅛ teaspoon vanilla extract
1½ tablespoons milk
¼ cup miniature chocolate chips

1. Make the cookies: In a small bowl, stir or whisk together the flour, baking powder, and salt. In a large bowl, cream the butter and sugar. Add the egg yolk, vanilla, milk, and melted chocolate and beat until well blended. Gradually add the flour mixture, blending well after each addition. Cover tightly and refrigerate for 1 hour, or until firm.

2. Place the dough on a piece of plastic wrap and shape it into a log 1½ to 2 inches in diameter. Wrap snugly in the plastic and refrigerate for 2 hours longer, or until very firm.

3. Preheat the oven to 350°F; have ready 1 or 2 ungreased baking sheets. Unwrap the log and use a sharp knife to cut it in an even number of ¼-inch-thick slices. Place the slices 1 inch apart on the prepared baking sheet.

4. Bake for 10 minutes. Transfer immediately to wire racks to cool.

5. Make the filling: Cream the butter and sugar until smooth. Add the salt, peppermint extract, vanilla, and milk and beat again. Stir in the miniature chips.

6. Make the sandwiches: Turn half the cookies flat side up; divide the filling evenly among them and use a small spatula to spread the filling evenly. Top with the remaining cookies, flat side down. Press the cookies lightly so the sandwiches hold together.

- *Makes about 18 sandwiches*

Cookie Ornaments

Rich Chocolate Butter Cookies (page 74) and Chocolate–Sour Cream Sugar Cookies (page 86) make delightful ornaments to hang on a Christmas tree. Here's how to do it: First, cut the rolled dough with Christmas cookie cutters—bell, angel, star, tree, wreath, or any other favorites. Transfer the cookies to the baking sheet.

Before baking, use a plastic drinking straw to punch a hole near the top of each cookie. The holes should remain open during baking; if they don't, punch holes again as soon as you take the hot cookies out of the oven. When the cookies are cool, thread a piece of narrow ribbon or thin cord through each one and knot the ends. Hang on the tree.

Cookie ornaments have an old-fashioned charm that goes beyond the Christmas tree. Tie cookie cutter animals to an evergreen or grapevine wreath. Hang cookie cutter bells and stars from the mantelpiece. Line up cookie cutter snowfolks, boys and girls, on a shelf, chair rail, windowsill, or window ledge.

Cookie Press and Pastry Bag Cookies

A cookie press is a gadget composed of a tube (into which you pack the cookie dough), a variety of templates (small perforated disks) that fit on the end of the tube, and a pump-type or screw-type insert that pushes the dough down the tube, through the perforated disk, and onto your baking sheet. It's a magical process, because when you bake the oddly shaped pressed cookies, they melt and become hearts and butterflies and daisies.

A pastry bag (plastic or muslin, disposable or reusable) is wide at the top so it's easy to fill, and narrow at the bottom to accommodate a coupler and a metal decorating tip. The tips come in many different sizes and shapes.

Tip: If you're buying a new cookie press, I recommend the pump type; it's extremely easy to use.

Chocolate Meringue Kisses

This recipe yields lots of kisses—bite-size meringues made with a pastry bag fitted with a star-shaped tip. Eat them one at a time, or sandwich pairs of kisses together with a bit of Lemon Cream Filling (page 106) or Mint Buttercream (page 108). For fancier cookies, dip the pointed top of each kiss in glaze (any flavor; pages 119 to 123) and let the glaze firm up before serving.

3½ tablespoons cocoa powder
1 cup confectioners' sugar
5 egg whites
⅔ cup sugar

1. Preheat the oven to 300°F; grease and generously flour 4 baking sheets. Have ready a 12-inch pastry bag (decorating bag) with a #2D (½-inch) star tip. Sift the cocoa and confectioners' sugar together into a small bowl; mix well with a whisk.

2. In a large bowl, beat the egg whites until frothy, then add 2 tablespoons of the granulated sugar and beat until the egg whites are thick and smooth and stand in soft, glossy peaks. Add all the remaining sugar and beat again for several minutes until the egg whites are very thick and glossy; they should hold soft peaks and soft ridges (from the beaters). Quickly fold in the cocoa mixture. The egg whites will deflate somewhat.

3. Fill the pastry bag with meringue mixture and pipe 1-inch-diameter kisses, ½ inch apart, onto the prepared baking sheet. Repeat with the remaining meringue, using as many baking sheets as needed.

4. Bake 2 sheets at a time (1 sheet on the middle shelf of the oven and the other sheet on the shelf above the middle) for 65 minutes, reversing their positions after 30 minutes; if the meringues are browning, reduce the oven temperature to 250°. Gently twist the meringues off the baking sheet or remove carefully with a small spatula if necessary. Brush excess flour off the bottoms.

Repeat the baking procedure with the kisses on the remaining baking sheets.

- *Makes about 200 kisses*

Chocolate-Dipped Mocha Thumbs

❦

This recipe makes a lot of cookies, but each delicate "thumb" is no more than a mouthful, so you'll need a lot of them. Great for parties and other elegant occasions.

2¼ cups flour
2 tablespoons cocoa powder
½ teaspoon baking powder
¼ teaspoon salt
1 cup (2 sticks) unsalted butter,
   at room temperature
¾ cup sugar
1 egg

1½ teaspoons vanilla extract
3 tablespoons strong coffee
   (1 teaspoon instant coffee stirred
   into 3 tablespoons boiling water)
4 ounces semisweet chocolate, chopped
2 teaspoons neutral vegetable oil
   (corn, safflower, canola, or sunflower)

1. Preheat the oven to 350°F; have ready 1 or 2 ungreased baking sheets. You will also need a cookie press fitted with a disk like the one in the illustration. If necessary, use a different disk (such as a heart), keeping in mind that you will be dipping 1 side of the baked cookie in chocolate glaze.

In a small bowl, stir or whisk together the flour, cocoa, baking powder and salt.

2. In a large bowl, cream the butter and sugar. Add the egg, vanilla, and coffee and beat until well blended. Gradually add the flour mixture, blending well after each addition.

3. Pack dough into the cookie press. Press the dough into the ungreased baking sheet, leaving 1 inch between cookies. Repeat, using the remaining dough.

4. Bake for 8 minutes. The hot cookies are fragile, so let them cool on the baking sheet for 3 to 4 minutes before transferring carefully to wire racks to finish cooling.

5. In a small, heavy saucepan over very low heat, melt the chocolate and oil, stirring until smooth to make a glaze. Put the glaze in a small bowl. Carefully dip 1 end of each thumb-shaped cookie in the melted chocolate, gently wiping off the excess chocolate on the edge of the bowl. Set the cookies aside on waxed paper to let the glaze firm up, which will take several hours at room temperature or about 15 minutes in the refrigerator.

- *Makes about 8 dozen cookies*

A Gift of Cookies

Try one of these pretty packaging ideas the very next time you offer a present of freshly baked chocolate cookies.

• Shiny paper sack or small shiny paper shopping bag: Line with white tissue paper, add the cookies, and close the top with stickers. If you like, decorate with more stickers and a bow.

• Basket, bowl, baking pan, small metal or plastic bucket: Line with a big piece of clear or colored cellophane. Stack the cookies on the cellophane, bring the cellophane up, and gather it over the cookies. Secure with a twist tie and cover the twist tie with ribbon and bow.

• Clear glass or plastic jar: Fill with cookies. Top with a pinked round of fabric; tie with gold cord, yarn, or grosgrain ribbon.

• Gift box: Choose white or a bright color. Line with white tissue paper, layer with cookies (with waxed paper between layers), and pop the lid on. Tie with inexpensive gift ribbon or satin ribbon.

• Cookie tin: Pick a tin in a solid color or printed with a pretty pattern. Line with plastic wrap, fill with cookies (with waxed paper between layers), and cover snugly. Top with a paper doily, wrap ribbon, and make a bow. Tuck a few silk flowers or a sprig of holly under the bow.

• Plastic container: Try a square, rectangular, or round kitchen container or a clear plastic shoebox. Fill with cookies, wrap simply with wide gingham ribbon, and tuck in a small extra—cinnamon sticks, pair of wooden spoons, nutmeg grater, candy canes, cookie cutter.

Chocolate Spritz Cookies

Crunchy, tasty spritz cookies are especially popular at Christmastime, so this recipe makes a generous amount. Freeze half for unexpected guests or mail a tinful to your relatives—spritz cookies last well and ship well. Experiment with a variety of disks to find the shapes you like best. ***Tip:*** These are especially easy to make because the baking sheets are used *ungreased*.

¾ cup (1½ sticks) unsalted butter,
   at room temperature
1½ cups sugar
1 egg
1 egg yolk
1 teaspoon vanilla extract

3 tablespoons milk
3 cups flour stirred with
   ¾ teaspoon salt
3 ounces unsweetened chocolate,
   melted and cooled

1. Preheat the oven to 350°F; have ready several ungreased baking sheets and a cookie press fitted with your choice of disk.

2. In a large bowl, cream the butter and sugar. Add the egg, egg yolk, vanilla, and milk and beat until well blended. Add half the flour and blend well. Add the melted chocolate and blend well. Add the remaining flour mixture and blend again.

3. Pack the dough into the cookie press. Press the dough into the ungreased baking sheet, leaving 1 inch between cookies.

4. Bake for 10 to 11 minutes; a cooled cookie should be crisp all the way through. Let the cookies cool for 1 minute on the baking sheet, then transfer to wire racks to finish cooling.

• *Makes about 10 dozen cookies*

Glazes

Glaze puts a lovely finishing touch on your cookies. There are many ways to use it—see *Fancy Tricks with Glaze: Dipping* (page 124) and *Fancy Tricks with Glaze: Drizzling or Spreading* (page 67) for a few ideas.

Keep in mind that glaze applied to cookies can take quite a while to firm up, especially in hot or humid weather; if you're in a hurry, refrigerate the glazed cookies and the glaze will harden quickly.

Vanilla Glaze

1½ tablespoons unsalted butter, melted
1½ teaspoons vanilla extract
¼ cup milk

2 pinches of salt
2 cups sifted confectioners' sugar

Stir together the melted butter, vanilla, milk, and salt. Add the confectioners' sugar and beat for about 4 minutes.

This glaze sets and dries quickly. To prevent a crust from forming, cover the unused portion with a piece of plastic wrap pressed directly onto the surface of the glaze.

If the glaze is too thin for your purpose, beat in a bit more sifted confectioners' sugar; if it is too thick, add a little more milk.

- *Makes about 1 cup*

Semisweet Chocolate Glaze

2 ounces unsweetened chocolate, chopped
¼ cup (½ stick) unsalted butter
6 tablespoons heavy cream

1 teaspoon vanilla extract
2 cups sifted confectioners' sugar,
or 1½ cups for a thin glaze

1. Melt the chocolate and butter either in a medium-size bowl resting on a saucepan holding a few inches of simmering water or in a saucepan large enough to contain all the ingredients. Stir until smooth. Turn off the heat.

2. Add the remaining ingredients and beat with a wire whisk until smooth. The glaze will thicken as it cools, so either leave the bowl of glaze in place on the pan of hot water until needed or reheat the glaze in the heavy saucepan over very low heat.

- *Makes about 1½ cups*

Mocha Glaze

2 ounces unsweetened chocolate,
   chopped
2 tablespoons butter

¼ cup strong coffee
½ teaspoon vanilla extract
1⅓ cups sifted confectioners' sugar

In a small saucepan over low heat, stir the chocolate and butter until blended. Transfer to a large bowl, add the coffee and vanilla, and stir again. Add the confectioners' sugar and beat until smooth. If necessary, thin with a little more coffee or thicken with a little more confectioners' sugar.

- *Makes about 1 cup*

Bittersweet Chocolate Glaze

---

3 ounces unsweetened chocolate, chopped
6 ounces semisweet chocolate, chopped
4 teaspoons neutral vegetable oil (corn, safflower, canola, or sunflower)

Melt the chocolate and oil in a heavy saucepan over very low heat, stirring until smooth.

- *Makes about 1 cup*

Fancy Tricks with Glaze: Dipping

Jazz up your completely cooled cookies with Vanilla Glaze (page 120), Semisweet Chocolate Glaze (page 121), Mocha Glaze (page 122) or Bittersweet Chocolate Glaze (page 123). *Tip:* For easy dipping, your glaze may need to be thinned slightly with water or whatever liquid is used in the recipe.

• Mounded drop cookies (such as Chocolate–Chocolate Chip Cookies, page 14, or Chocolate Snickerdoodles, page 19) can be dipped head first in warm glaze. Set cookies right side up on waxed paper until the glaze is firm.

• Flat cookies (such as Chocolate Shortbread, page 68, or any of the icebox cookies, pages 89 to 101) or molded cookies (such as Tender Chocolate-Almond Crescents, page 50, or Chocolate Biscotti with Pistachios, page 52) can be dipped edgewise in warm glaze. Dip half the cookie, 1 end or both ends, then let excess glaze drip off. Set aside on waxed paper until the glaze is firm and dry.

• If you like, add an extra: Immediately after dipping a cookie in glaze, dip the glazed part in sprinkles (chocolate or colored), finely chopped nuts, or toasted coconut. Be sure to choose an extra that's appropriate for the cookie.

Magic Mocha

On the theory that you can't have too much of a good thing, try this refreshing iced chocolate drink that goes perfectly with summer and chocolate cookies. To make 1 glass of Magic Mocha, stir *1 teaspoon cocoa powder* and *2 teaspoons sugar* together in a glass. Add *⅓ cup hot coffee* and stir to dissolve the sugar. Add *⅓ cup milk or half-and-half* and mix well. Add ice and enjoy.

Dessert and Cookies

Pair fruit, sorbet, or pudding with homemade chocolate cookies to create an easy dessert for a family or company dinner.

Strawberries and cream
Chocolate Meringue Kisses / 112

•

Wedges of cantaloupe or honeydew
Chocolate Biscotti with Pistachios / 52

•

Fresh raspberries or blueberries
Chocolate Cups I or II (62 and 64)

•

Sliced peaches or nectarines
Chocolate-Almond Sandies / 76

•

Watermelon
Chocolate Pretzels / 48

•

Cubes of ripe pineapple
Chocolate-Coconut Macaroons / 24

Sliced mango, starfruit, and papaya
Chocolate Sandwiches with Mint Buttercream Filling / 108

•

Bananas sautéed with butter and brown sugar
Cocoa Crisps / 94

•

Baked apples
Chocolate-Oatmeal Crispies / 15

•

Poached pears
Chocolate-Dipped Mocha Thumbs / 114

•

Vanilla pudding
Chocolate-Cherry Squares with Mini-Chip Frosting / 34

•

Rice pudding
Chocolate-Orange Icebox Cookies / 90

•

Raspberry or other sorbet
Chocolate–Sour Cream Sugar Cookies / 86

•

Vanilla ice cream, ice milk, or frozen yogurt
Tender Chocolate-Almond Crescents / 50

•

Fruit salad
One-Bowl Fudgies / 41

Index